LEE RAINWATER was born in Oxford, Mississippi, and studied at the University of Chicago. He is the author of *Workingman's Wife, Family Design,* and *The Moynihan Report and the Politics of Controversy,* as well as numerous articles. He is at present Professor of Sociology and Anthropology at Washington University, St. Louis.

And the Poor Get Children

And the Poor Get Children

Sex, Contraception, and Family Planning in the Working Class

By **LEE RAINWATER**

Assisted by **KAROL KANE WEINSTEIN**

Preface by J. MAYONE STYCOS

COLLEGE FOR HUMAN SERVICES
LIBRARY
345 HUDSON STREET
NEW YORK, N.Y. 10014

GREENWOOD PRESS, PUBLISHERS
WESTPORT, CONNECTICUT

Library of Congress Cataloging in Publication Data

Rainwater, Lee.
 And the poor get children.

 Reprint. Originally published: Chicago : Quadrangle
Books, 1967, c1960. (Quadrangle paperbacks)
 Bibliography: p.
 Includes index.
 1. Birth control--United States. 2. Labor and
laboring classes--United States. I. Weinstein,
Karol Kane. II. Title.
HQ766.5.U5R3 1984   304.6'6'0973   84-12770
ISBN 0-313-24452-9 (lib. bdg.)

© 1960 by Social Research, Inc.
Originally published in 1960 by Quadrangle Books, Inc.

Reprinted with the permission of Franklin Watts, Inc.

Reprinted in 1984 by Greenwood Press
A division of Congressional Information Service, Inc.
88 Post Road West, Westport, Connecticut 06881

Printed in the United States of America

10 9 8 7 6 5 4 3 2 1

PREFACE

DEMOGRAPHIC STUDIES in Europe and the United States long ago demonstrated that the upper social classes evidence lower rates of fertility than do the lower classes. Studies conducted earlier in this century then proved fairly conclusively that such differentials were largely the product of variations in contraceptive behavior. It is a curious fact that our knowledge has progressed but little from this point. Planned Parenthood and other groups have sponsored a good deal of research concerning the relative efficiency of various contraceptives, but these have proven merely what most people had suspected —that almost any method used faithfully will greatly reduce fertility. The basic problem, important both in a theoretical and practical sense, of what leads more people of one class to practice family limitation and to practice it more faithfully than those of another remained unanswered.

The famous Indianapolis study was a step in this direction. It was aimed primarily at the question of explaining differential fertility and family planning behavior in terms of social and psychological factors. In confining the sample to urban native white Protestant women of at least eight years of education, the study deliberately attempted to minimize the impact of social class and other broad social characteristics. But even within this relatively homogeneous sample, social class proved to be the most powerful predictor of family planning behavior—so much so, indeed, that most of the social and psychological characteristics added little in the way of explanation.

The authors of that study were unusually candid in providing plausible explanations for the failure of the research to add in any crucial way to our knowledge of the social and psychological correlates of fertility behavior. It is all the more curious, therefore, that there is no mention, to my knowledge, of an extraordinary omission—sex.

In the Indianapolis questionnaire of over 1000 items, only one small question on attitudes toward sexual relations was included, and as one reads the hundreds of pages of careful and often ingenious analysis, one gets the impression that contraceptive practices have nothing to do with sexual relations. Moreover, when thirty-five experts gathered to discuss the study and to explore the possibilities for new studies, although everything from neuropsychiatric inventories to factorial designs was proposed, not one expert discussed the importance of gathering data in the sexual sphere.*

We must conclude that the collection of sexual data has been regarded as either irrelevant or impossible. With regard to the latter view, the myth that only clinical or anthropological techniques can elicit intimate sexual data has lived with social scientists for a long time, and still lingers on despite various demonstrations to the contrary. Thus, in the most recent and comprehensive study of contraceptive behavior in the United States, a questionnaire of over 100 items still contained none on sexual relations, and the investigators apparently felt that even the questions on contraceptives could not be asked directly by the interviewers. Instead, cards listing various contraceptives were handed to the respondent and she was asked to reply by a code designation. The authors appear somewhat surprised that virtually no difficulty was encountered

---

* The proceedings are reported by C. V. Kiser in "Exploration of Possibilities for New Studies of Factors Affecting Size of Family," *Milbank Memorial Fund Quarterly*, Oct. 1953.

in getting respondents to talk freely about such matters, and that some respondents found income questions more personal than those relating to family planning.*

Dr. Rainwater's investigations leave little doubt that extraordinarily rich sexual data can be gathered by professional interviewers. Although the author gives us only the barest of insights into the interviewing and sampling problems, the abundant quotations show clearly that the respondents were willing to speak freely and at length about intimate matters.

But of greater importance is the fact that the present study begins to fill in some of the anomalous gaps left by earlier investigations. It places contraceptive behavior and attitudes squarely within a context of sexual behavior and attitudes which in turn is placed in a context of social class. For illustrative purposes let us consider the areas of knowledge of and attitudes toward sex on the part of lower class women.

The lower classes are usually assumed to be much more permissive about sexual behavior than the upper classes, and it is therefore commonly believed that members of this class know a great deal about sex before marriage. By way of contrast, in the present sample, "quite a few women (before marriage) . . . did not know that . . . conception comes about as a result of sexual intercourse," and the degree of current misinformation concerning the processes of fertilization is startling indeed.

Another common assumption is that lower-class women are less repressed about sex; but the present study shows that a high proportion of them are indifferent to or repelled by sexual relations. Dr. Rainwater attempts to tie together the misinformation and negative attitudes toward sex with knowledge of and attitudes toward contraception. One way in which these variables interact is beautifully illustrated by a woman who remarked, "The

---

* Freedman, R., P. K. Whelpton and A. A. Campbell, *Family Planning, Sterility and Population Growth* (N. Y.: McGraw-Hill, 1959).

Doctor told me about all that stuff but I was too ashamed to listen."

Critical readers will raise the important question of the extent to which the patterns here described as lower-class American are equally characteristic of other social classes and other societies. Unfortunately, studies of this kind are rare, but what evidence exists suggests that the major phenomena described may indeed be class-linked. The chief study of relevance is the Kinsey volume on the American female.* We cite below six important findings from Kinsey's study which are consistent with the general tenor of the present study and which are contrary to "common sense" beliefs:

1. American women in lower educational groups do not have sex relations more frequently than higher educated women.
2. The lower the educational level the less likely it is that pre-marital relations occurred.
3. Attitudes toward nudity are more conservative among lower class women.
4. Erotic arousal "from any source" is lowest among the women of least education.
5. Fewer women in the lower educational groups have ever reached orgasm in marriage.
6. The frequency of achievement of orgasm is considerably less among the more poorly-educated women.

It would seem, in sort, that fewer of the good things of life are free than has commonly been supposed. The lower classes seem underprivileged not only in terms of sexual knowledge but, at least by several measures, in terms of sexual gratification as well.

It is also of interest that the only published study parallel to Rainwater's done in another culture (this writer's *Family and Fertility in Puerto Rico*†) produced strikingly

---

* C. Kinsey, W. B. Pomeroy, C. R. Martin, and P. H. Gebhard, *Sexual Behavior in the Human Female* (Phila.: W. B. Saunders, 1953).

† J. M. Stycos, *Family and Fertility in Puerto Rico* (N. Y.: Columbia Univ. Press, 1955).

PREFACE   [xi]

similar findings regarding attitudes toward and knowledge of sex. At the time I believed that the female rejection of sexuality and the predominant ignorance of sexual matters was primarily a *cultural* phenomenon; but Kinsey's data and those of the present study suggest the utility of a class hypothesis which may cut across a number of cultures.

When research on the oral contraceptive tablet was initiated some years ago, it was soon discovered that many basic physiological "facts of life" were still unknown, and a great deal of research was then routed in this direction. Perhaps there is a growing awareness now that we know even less about the social "facts of life," and that sexual and contraceptive behavior may have a few things in common. In sponsoring this study, Planned Parenthood has shown a refreshing shift in research emphasis away from "efficiency studies" of contraception and toward a serious concern with the human factor. We should not lose sight of the fact, however, that this study is based on a sample of 46 men and 50 women. Because of its great promise, we sincerely hope that the present investigation will not be interred in the ever-expanding graveyard of "exploratory studies" whose tantalizing hypotheses are indefinitely left in limbo.

J. MAYONE STYCOS

Cornell University

ACKNOWLEDGMENTS

THIS STUDY was conducted for the Planned Parenthood Federation of America, Inc., by Social Research, Inc. We are grateful to Planned Parenthood for their support of the research and for their encouragement to us in our expansion of the original report into this published form. The findings and interpretations reported here, however, are the sole responsibility of the researchers, and should not be taken as reflecting the policies or points of view of Planned Parenthood.

The first stage of the study was carried out by Karol Kane Weinstein under the direction of Lee Rainwater, who later analyzed the data and prepared this statement of our findings. Many of the ideas incorporated in the final version were developed by Mrs. Weinstein, but final responsibility for the statements contained in this book rests with the principal author.

Dr. Sidney J. Levy consulted with us throughout the course of the study and contributed particularly to the discussion of the personality characteristics of effective and ineffective contraceptive users in chapter v. Mrs. Bobette Adler Levy provided us with material concerning psychopathological aspects of contraceptive practice based on interviews with psychotherapists and gynecologists; this material was especially helpful in developing hypotheses to be tested with our data. Dr. Benjamin D. Wright assisted us in the statistical analysis of some of the interview material. We were aided in other ways by Drs.

Ira O. Glick and Richard Coleman, by Mr. Gerald Handel of the staff of Social Research, Inc., and by one of the organization's consultants, Professor Martin B. Loeb.

Any research dependent on interviews owes its largest debt to the individuals who give their time as respondents; in this case the debt is particularly great because the subjects discussed were intimate and made heavy demands on the respondents for honesty and forthrightness. We are grateful to the field department of Social Research, Inc., Mrs. Leone Phillips, Hanna Bratman and Marion Thompson, for supervising the collection of interviews, and to the interviewers who conducted these long and difficult conversations with respondents: Messrs. E. F. Eggers, Robert Feher, Burrill Freedman, David Hanan, Phillip Marcus, L. N. Max and Saville Sax, Miss Adelaide Bean, and Mrs. Fay Borkan, Rena Cherney, M. Cornwall, Rose Cummins, Dorothy Eaton, Pearl Hoopes, Myrna Jacobs, Susan Lahm, J. Lessman, Mary Miller, Agnes Nerode, Shirlee Sher and Shirley Wagner.

Three persons read our manuscript critically, and their suggestions have been very helpful in clarifying our findings: Miss Margaret Snyder, Professor Mozell C. Hill, and Dr. Christopher Tietze. Their encouragement has been a central factor in this publication. We are also indebted to Mr. Alexander J. Morin of Quadrangle Books, Inc., for his help in editing the manuscript in ways that simplify communication. We must assume the responsibility for the shortcomings that still exist.

Finally, I wish to thank my wife, Carol Kampel Rainwater, for her encouragement and forbearance during the writing of this book, and for her concrete contribution in preparing the index.

LEE RAINWATER

Chicago, Illinois

CONTENTS

	Preface	vii
	Acknowledgments	xiii
1	Introduction	1
2	"Doing Nothing Is the Easiest Way Out"	9
3	Patterns of Family Planning Behavior	19
4	Assumptions and Orientations in Family Planning	44
5	Social Role and Self-Concept in the Marital Relationship	60
6	Mutuality and Rejection in Sexual Relations	92
7	Sexual Relations, Family Planning, and Contraception	122
8	Contraceptive Practice: Methods and Meanings	142
9	℞ for Family Planning in the Working Class	167
APPENDIX A	The Acceptability of Contraceptive Methods to their Users, BY MARY S. CALDERONE, M.D.	180
APPENDIX B	Note on Research Procedures	185
	References	191
	Index	197

And the Poor Get Children

chapter i

INTRODUCTION

> It cannot be denied that contraceptive measures become a necessity in married life at some time or other, and theoretically it would be one of the greatest triumphs of mankind, one of the most tangible liberations from the bondage of nature to which we are subject, were it possible to raise the responsible act of procreation to the level of a voluntary and intentional act. and to free it from its entanglement with an indispensable satisfaction of a natural desire.
>
> *Sigmund Freud*, 1898

THROUGHOUT HUMAN HISTORY, political and religious leaders, philosophers, and scientists have concerned themselves with the problems of human fertility and population growth. For over a century, dedicated men and women have sought to deal with these problems in practical ways by fostering the use of contraceptives and by teaching the logic and value of consciously-formulated family planning. Modern technology has made available to us the means to realize family planning goals, and in many parts of the world large segments of society have adopted one or another contraceptive practice that enables them to hold their families to some desired size.

Today we have been made highly aware of population size by the realization that medical and nutritional advances throughout the world carry with them the danger of a too-rapid increase in population. Because of a falling death rate, it may not be possible for the human community to take advantage of the healthier and more abundant life that technological advances should make possible. The "population bomb" has come to seem as much a threat to the human condition as the more directly lethal nuclear weapons.

The most serious problems are, of course, faced in the less industrialized, underdeveloped countries that are only now beginning to experience the benefits of modern public health measures. In these areas, progress in medical science creates an explosive population growth that could make impossible both economic and social development (Meier, 1959).

Population growth has a macrocosmic and a microcosmic aspect. A society's population problem is made up of the little population problems of countless specific families who have more children than their resources can support adequately. The sum of all of these individual problems can be an acute problem for the society. However, when excess births are confined to a small proportion of families, we may have instead the more circumscribed social problem of these particular families' difficulties in maintaining a reasonable standard of living. Such is the situation in the United States: most of the population manages to have roughly the number of children they desire; proportionately few families, but enough to create real social concern, have more children than they really want or can support.

In this country, the problem of having more children than are wanted or can be adequately supported is largely confined to persons of one social group—a fact immortalized in the hyperbolic phrase, "The rich get richer and the poor get children." As family limitation has become an increasingly rational process, the middle class has been able to limit family size quite effectively in terms of whatever goals its members set for themselves. Traditionally and in reality, it is the poor people—the "working class," the "lower class,"—who have too many children.

To say that working class people more often have a

greater number of children than they want is not to say that middle class people never have the same problem, never experience "excess fertility." Certainly a large number of middle class couples complete their families with more children than they might have preferred. However, on a proportionate basis, middle class couples much less often have what they admit to themselves are "too many" children. Working class women are particularly often forced to face the fact that the number of children they have makes life much more difficult than it might be.

The reader must also keep clearly in mind that when we speak of a couple having "too many children," we mean this in terms of their own conscious desires. If a couple says to themselves and to our interviewer that they want four children, we must accept that statement as valid for them. An objective observer may say that they cannot really afford four children, either financially or psychically, but that is a judgment of a different order. A population expert may say that the United States cannot afford so many families with four children, even if they want them, but this really raises a different question from the one investigated here. While it may be true that there is genuine reason for alarm at the possibility of a U.S. population of 312 million in the year 2000 and of 600 million in 2050, even if all the babies who contribute to these numbers are wanted, such a concern requires research that deals with quite different questions than the ones we raise here in connection with the psychosocial dynamics of effective contraceptive practice.

As used in this study, the term "working class" has a very specific meaning: it defines a group of people who conform to a number of criteria based on many investigations into social class structure. To the social scientist, the working class is composed of those families who occupy a particular social position which is the product of a particular economic and occupational status, of particular educational attainments, of living in particular kinds of neighborhoods, and of a particular style of life (Warner and Lunt, 1941). In these families, the breadwinners work in manual, "blue-collar" occupations or lower-level service jobs. Their incomes are, on the average, lower than those of higher-status people, although our current prosperity and the success of trade unionism have tended to erase this difference. Working class people generally live in neighborhoods regarded as not very desirable, and their housing is modest. High school graduation represents their greatest educational attainment, and many working-class people leave school before graduating. The group defined by these characteristics is, of course, large. Over half our country's population falls into this social class.

The working class itself can be further divided into two sub-groups according to social status and related ways of life. *The upper-lower class* includes the larger portion of the group and is characterized by greater prosperity and stability. Upper-lower class workers generally are in semi-skilled and medium-skilled work; they are in manual occupations or in responsible but not highly regarded service jobs such as policemen, firemen, or bus drivers. They have generally had at least some high school education. Their families live in reasonably comfortable housing, in neighborhoods composed mainly of other manual and lower-level service workers. Although people in this group tend today to regard themselves as living the good life of average Americans, they are still aware that they do not have as much social status or prestige as the middle class white-collar worker or the highly-skilled technician and factory foreman.

The lower-lower class represents approximately one-quarter of the working class and about 15 per cent of the total population of the United States. The people in this group are very much aware that they do not participate fully in the good life of the average American; they feel at the "bottom of the heap" and consider themselves at a disadvantage in seeking the goods that the society has to offer. They generally work at unskilled jobs, and often they work only intermittently or are chronically unemployed. Few people in this group graduate from high school, and a great many go no further than grammar school. They live in slum and near-slum neighborhoods, and their housing tends to be cramped and deteriorated. Although many earn fairly good wages when they work ($75 to $100 per week is not uncommon), the seasonal or intermittent nature of their jobs and their relatively impulsive spending habits often prevent them from maintaining what most Americans regard as a decent standard of living.

The distinction between these two levels of the working class is of considerable importance in further defining the group afflicted with excess births. Although upper-lower class couples do not show the same rationality and early family planning as middle class couples, they usually manage to limit their families, through the use of contraception, to a size they regard as desirable. Lower-lower class couples, however, are not nearly so effective at family limitation and much more often feel burdened by having more children than they want. Because this differentiation between upper-lower and lower-lower class is of considerable importance in understanding successes and failures in family limitation, we will frequently call attention to differences between the two status groups in the analysis which follows. Also, when quotations are given from an interview, we will usually indicate whether the respondent was in the upper-lower or the lower-lower class.

The reader unfamiliar with social class terminology needs to be warned against some reactions he may have. In the United States we do not easily face up to the facts of social hierarchy and differences in social prestige; our official ideology tells us that all men are, or should be, equal. Yet in our daily lives we behave in terms of differences of status between people of differing financial, educational, or social attainments. Placement of people in classes by an examination of these characteristics is not meant to be invidious: we are not saying that the lower-lower person is somehow not as "good" as the upper-lower, or the latter less "good" than the middle-class individual. Rather, we use these terms as descriptive of the positions individuals occupy in the social hierarchy and as indicative of particular ways of life and personal propensities that generally go with such positions. Similarly, it is incumbent on the reader who wishes fully to understand the findings reported here to lay aside his more personal feelings about the behavior and values we deal with and to avoid making the normal cultural equation between "lower" in the social hierarchy and lower in a "moral" sense. He should also bear in mind that by examining some of the more nonadaptive and unconstructive aspects of working class life as they bear on family planning we do not mean to damn the individuals so characterized, any more than the physician seeks to damn his patient by describing malfunctions of the body.

Our study deals with the background of social and psychological factors which influence the ways in which working class people think about family planning and contraception. It is important to understand these background factors, since a simple knowledge of what these people do is not enough to understand their behavior, to predict how they might behave in the future, or to influence their behavior in the direction of more rational family planning. As Margaret Mead notes (1949), behind the various maneuvers people in all societies make toward family limitation, "there lies a subtler factor, a willingness or an unwillingness to breed that is deeply imbedded in the character structure of both men and women. . . . Beneath population trends that are registered in statistics, behind articulate anxieties as to the size of the village fighting force or hunting party, or the shrinking amount of land available for each child, there lie the developed attitudes of men and women towards child-bearing." And, we should add, their developed attitudes toward ways to avoid child-bearing.

This study is an initial effort toward understanding these factors as they apply to urban working-class people in this country. It is a pilot study involving intensive interviews with ninety-six working class men and women; the sample and the methods used are described in Appendix B. The study raises more questions than it answers; it simply begins the necessary exploration of what lies behind the descriptive facts of contraceptive use patterns. However, as will be apparent in the chapters that follow, this examination of working class actions, attitudes, and motives proceeds from a fairly solid base of other research about lower class lives and personality, research which provides a context for our examination of family planning and contraception.*

In recent years, social class analysis of this kind has been applied to a number of public health problems; our work is paralleled by studies of mental disease (Hollingshead and Redlich, 1958; Myers and Roberts, 1959), of psychosomatic illness (Ruesch, 1946, 1951), and of maternal health and child care (Boek and others, 1957). All these researchers take as their point of departure the assumption that a fuller understanding of personality and style of life in particular social classes will facilitate an understanding of the psychosocial dynamics of the public health problem in question.

In the chapters that follow we will examine the patterns of family planning and limitation that occur in

―――――――

* This study is an extension of our earlier research on working class life (Rainwater, 1956; Rainwater, Coleman and Handel, 1959). Our studies have drawn heavily on the work of W. Lloyd Warner and his colleagues (1941, 1944, 1949, 1953) and of Allison Davis and his co-workers (1941, 1946, 1947, 1948). We have also been encouraged by the many similarities between the picture of American working class life presented in these studies and that of English working class life given by various writers (Hogarth, 1957; Slater and Woodside, 1951; Spinley, 1953; and Young and Willmott, 1957).

the working class and probe into the underlying assumptions and value orientations that working class people reveal when they talk about family planning. Then we will show how their behavior is related to certain patterns of relationships between husband and wife and between parents and their children. Sexual behavior, while only one part of the marital relationship, is of sufficient importance in conditioning contraceptive practice to be treated separately in two chapters. After this analysis of background factors, we turn to the attitudes and meanings that condition the use or non-use of particular contraceptive methods. (Although our study covers the major contraceptive methods, one frequent method of family limitation—abortion—is not discussed, because we did not risk the high refusal rates that would result from questions about so emotion-laden a topic.) Finally, we suggest some implications of our results for public health programs concerned with contraception and planned parenthood, and we look at the degree of congruence between our findings concerning working class Americans and the findings of those who have studied family planning in other cultures—India, Japan, Puerto Rico, and Jamaica.

First, however, let us look at the issues of family planning and contraception at the most concrete and humanly specific level by examining the matter as it is dealt with by one particular working class couple. The Chicago couple we will call the Nelsons demonstrate in their comments (quoted in the next chapter) the kind of information collected in our interviews with forty-six men and fifty women in Chicago and Cincinnati. Our respondents were selected to represent the two status groups that make up the working class; our interviews with them averaged two hours in length.

chapter ii

"DOING NOTHING IS THE EASIEST WAY OUT"

WHAT KIND OF PEOPLE have more children than they want? How do they live their lives so that after five years of marriage they already have more children than they can readily support and still cannot find a way of preventing further pregnancies? Arthur and Betty Nelson are only one such couple, but their story is instructive.

They have been married for five years and have five children. One is an illegitimate son aged seven whose father contributes to his support; there are also two other boys, one five years and the other seven months old, and two girls, four and three years old. Mr. Nelson is twenty-six years old and his wife is twenty-five. Listen to Betty Nelson as she tells her story:

"I wanted four children myself. He wants a real large family. I think at least two years between them would give the mother a better chance to train her children properly. She would have more time. My husband likes them close together so they all grow up together. They are better companions that way, he says. I don't think a family should have more children than they can take care of. We can't even take care of what we have now.

"I really don't mind having children, though. In fact when I am pregnant is the only time I don't worry about getting that way. It is never a bad thing to me. I am sick a couple of months but then I feel fine. My husband is always pleased when I'm pregnant. I enjoy our relations so much more then. The satisfaction is that I don't worry about getting that way. I have never had any troubles in pregnancy or in childbirth either.

"We don't use any certain word for limiting, just what to do to keep from getting pregnant. What we have been using is the rhythm system. It works for a while, then we get careless. We take a chance when we know we shouldn't. There are several other methods we have heard of but not tried. My husband will not use rubbers; he says they hurt him, but I think he just doesn't want to use them. I have thought of going to a clinic for a diaphragm, but I'm real backward about doing that. I don't even go to the doctor to be examined when I'm pregnant. I never go until about a month before I have the baby.

"I didn't know anything about all this before I had a baby. After the second one was born, a nurse told me about the diaphragm and the safe period. So afterward we used the chart for the safe period for a while. That's all we ever used. My husband won't use anything at all. He wants a lot of children and he won't try very hard to keep from having them. He says if I don't want them then it's up to me to use the prevention. I think he should take the responsibility. It would be easier for him to use something. But it's getting to the place now where if he won't I'm going to have to because we have five already.

"I use a douche sometimes but have never tried that as a regular method. My husband wouldn't use withdrawal, that is one thing he says he just would not do. He doesn't believe in that. He says that would be worse than not doing it at all. I've heard people talk about the jellies and creams but they say they aren't sure protection. I have heard of some kind of suppositories you use inside before intercourse but I've never tried them either."

It quickly becomes apparent as Mrs. Nelson talks that

Arthur Nelson represents a large part of her problem. She feels that family limitation is strictly up to her, that she can expect no co-operation from her husband. What, then, is his version of their story?

"It doesn't make any difference to me how many we have. I like large families. I believe you always manage somehow even if you have a lot of children and they enjoy each other more. I think they should be close together—about one and one-half years apart is enough. I think if the mother is strong and healthy that's all that counts. I think a couple will have just what they should have. Maybe that's crazy but it is the way I feel. If you aren't supposed to have them, you won't; if you are, you will. Having children has never been too bad for my wife. She isn't sick very much and she never seems to mind it.

"When we talk about this, she says I'm crazy and I should do something to keep from getting her pregnant. She says we have enough now and should not have any more children. I just laugh at her and tell her if she isn't supposed to have them she won't get that way. I don't do anything about it myself. The only thing we have ever used was the safe period each month. I have been pretty careful about that but not careful enough, I guess. We haven't tried any other methods yet, but we have heard of several and have planned to try something.

"I didn't know anything about contraception before I was married, only to use rubbers, and that I just don't like to do so that's why I never used them. To tell you the truth I haven't learned much since I've been married. My wife thinks I should use rubbers or find something I can use so she won't have to get that way again. But I say that she is the one that should do something to protect herself. I think she should have the main responsibility because there are more different things a woman can do for protection.

"We have talked about the diaphragm. The nurse

at the hospital where the babies were born wanted my wife to be fitted for one, but she won't go. She says she's afraid to go. She really isn't afraid, she's just embarrassed. She sometimes uses a douche—puts something in it, vinegar or something. We've never used jellies or creams. We don't know much about them or if they would work. She said someone told her about suppositories but we have never used them."

The Nelsons illustrate a pattern of family planning that will be more fully described in the next chapter as one of sporadic and careless contraception. It is clear that this comes about through a conflict between the wife, who is beginning to feel desperately the need to limit her family, and the husband, who refuses to face the realities of their situation. What kind of people get themselves in such a dilemma?

The Nelsons are placed socially in the lower-lower class and are reasonably typical of couples in that group. Their apartment is an old converted house in a slum neighborhood next to the railroad tracks. Arthur Nelson has worked in a variety of unskilled and semi-skilled jobs since he got out of the army seven years ago, but the best-paying job he ever had was as a private while in service. Currently, the Nelsons live on public assistance and whatever odd jobs he can get. Mrs. Nelson worked as a waitress before her marriage, but not since. Neither has any religious affiliation because "we just never felt we could afford clothes and things fit for church."

First we might ask, "How did these two people happen to get married?" Mrs. Nelson tells the story:

"We have been married five years. We were both twenty-one when we got married. Neither of us had been married before. I might as well tell you, I had my oldest boy before I was married. In fact I had my first two before I was married, but I married the father of the second one. I was raped the first time I got pregnant. I was out with my girl friend and her boy friend.

We had been drinking, so when we started home he took her home first and on the way home he started getting smart with me. I got scared and started fighting him, then he hit me and beat me. I guess he must have knocked me out, then he raped me. That was the first time I ever had been touched and I got pregnant from it. I was afraid to say anything to anyone about it. No one knew it until I was three months gone. My folks had him arrested then, but I wouldn't marry him. He pays me five dollars a week for the boy's support and that's all I get.

"My aunt had told me all about the things that happen to girls when they had affairs with men. She told me when I was about fifteen years old that if a boy ever put that in me I would have a baby. So I was scared to death of doing that, and sure enough the first time it happened to me I got pregnant.

"I had known my husband all these years and had never gone with him. He was in the service when all of this happened to me. I went with his brother some time after this, then I started going with him. I fell in love with him right away, but my mother watched us so close and fussed at me so much. She wouldn't let us get married. So then I found out I was pregnant again, and I wouldn't marry him then even though he wanted me to. He was glad I was that way and thought now we could get married. But I wouldn't marry him until the baby was born. I said I didn't want him to see me while I was big with the baby. When the baby was two weeks old we got married. He loves children. My mother never knew about this because she died around that time. Then we moved in with father to take care of him and give us a place to live also."

Marriage began with quite a few problems. It is surprising, then, that Mr. Nelson feels as pleased as he does about his lot in life. He is not a worrier, as he tells us:

"I guess I'm a person that don't worry too much about things. I just sort of figure to let nature take its course. I love sports of all kinds.

"I think it's important for a husband to be a good lover because all women like to be loved and a good lover would also be a good father. A woman should be a good lover, too. Men also want to be loved and shown a lot of attention when he's home. She must also be a good lover to her children.

"About the only troubles we have are about money. We get along fine in every other way. When I'm out of work we argue sometimes about that. It is hard to keep up with our rent and other bills when I'm laid off, but we always manage. I just can't seem to get steady work. I don't know why, but it seems something always happens when I get a good job.

"We have had a lot of good times since we've been married, but we have had some bad times too. The children were all sick in the hospital at one time a couple of years ago, and we didn't know if they would live or not. They all got better, though. That is the only troubles we have had outside of my not being able to get steady work. [Note that he does not seem to feel any deep sense of failure about his poor job experiences.]

"My wife is pretty easy to get along with, I think. She is a slow, easy-going person. She doesn't like for me to drink or play the horses. She isn't interested in anything in particular. She doesn't care for sports too much, but I do. She is a good mother and she loves me a lot too. She does fuss at me sometimes when I don't shave. I don't like to shave."

Mr. Nelson feels that a steady job is all he needs to make life perfect, but he doesn't like the demands that steady jobs make, so "something always happens" when he does get employment. He is pleased with his wife and with the life he has away from work. In turn, Mrs. Nelson is pleased with her husband, and defines his job instability as somehow not really his fault. Actually, she feels equally inadequate in her own job as housekeeper:

"I guess I'm like most anyone else. I don't have any special interests. I just take care of the house and the kids. I guess I'm not too hard to get along with. I'm not a very good housekeeper. The kids keep the house so messed up I just don't even try to keep everything picked up.

"My biggest problems are financial because my husband is laid off so much. He works steady when he has a job, but he doesn't seem to be able to stay at one place for very long at a time. We had a lot of trouble too with the children being sick for a while. Two years ago in February we had three of the children in the hospital at one time, two of them with pneumonia and one with asthma. We didn't know if they were going to pull through or not. That was really a bad time, but they all got all right and things have been pretty good as far as sickness goes ever since. My husband and I have never had any trouble to speak of between ourselves. We get along all right.

"He has a wonderful personality, full of fun. He laughs a lot and is always teasing me about something. When I get mad at him about something he just stands and laughs at me. The madder I get the more he laughs. So he is a person you just can't stay mad at. He likes sports of all kinds—baseball, football, fishing, car and horse races. He likes to bet on the horses. I fuss at him about that, but it doesn't do any good. If he has some money he will do it. He is a very affectionate person. He likes to make over me and he likes to love me a lot. We play around a lot. He gets me up on his shoulder and carries me around and things like that. His good points are that he's jolly and good-natured—easy to get along with. He gets along fine with the children.

"He helps me around the house a lot when he's not working. He likes to be with me and the children, so if I have work to do he helps me so we can be together. He helps me clean, wash, iron, everything, he even loves to cook. We get along fine."

It is clear that coasting along, doing nothing, is a very attractive way of dealing with problems for this couple. Mr. Nelson insists on doing little to solve the problems that confront the family; Mrs. Nelson goes along because she cannot bring herself to be forceful and insistent with him. She feels very dependent upon him for affection and for stability in her life; she will not readily threaten this by demands she fears he will not or cannot meet.

In their discussions of sexual relationships these needs come strongly to the fore. Betty Nelson tells us:

"Well, our sexual relationship is real good I would say. We both enjoy it very much. We only have relations about two or sometimes three times a week. We don't both go to bed at the same time, I guess. I like to go to bed early myself. He likes to sit up late and watch the late movie on TV, so I'm sleeping when he comes to bed, usually. He isn't too aware of my desires, I don't think, because I never say anything or let him know when I feel like I want to. I just go to bed, but I guess he doesn't think that's the reason I go. I am very aware of his desires because he always starts loving me up and playing around. I know when he does he wants something. Things haven't changed; they've been the same since we were first married. I think sexual relations are very important; they make me feel good. I feel like I would like to more often, but my husband doesn't go to bed when I do and by the time he comes to bed I'm always asleep. They could be better for me if I didn't have to worry so much about getting pregnant. We would probably do it more if I didn't have to worry about that.

"Sex is very important to my husband. He says they give him the feeling of perfect relaxation. He always wants to go right to sleep afterwards. He says he sleeps better then than at any other time. I think my husband enjoys it the most. But it's important to both of us. He seems to get a more relaxed feeling out of it than I do because he falls asleep right away. I always have to get right up and go to the bathroom and after that I don't seem to have that relaxed feeling he does. I guess it is because I do have to get up right away, I never thought of that before. It's possible that could be why he enjoys it so much more. He doesn't have to get up right away and do something. I get as much enjoyment out of it as he does at the time, I have to think right away of getting up and doing something so I won't get pregnant."

Even in sexual relations, she feels somewhat frustrated because her husband often does not desire intercourse when she does and because after intercourse he withdraws into sleep, leaving her feeling isolated and uneasy. It is understandable that, with her need for this kind of intimate contact, she is reluctant to assert herself with her husband about contraception and thus run the risk of alienating him.

For his part, Arthur Nelson finds sexual relations highly meaningful, but he is not able to reconcile his own desire for unobstructed pleasure with his wife's concern about pregnancy. He appreciates his wife's problem, but he does nothing more about it than protest his good intentions:

"Our sexual relations are fine. We enjoy it about the same most of the time. We have relations two or three times a week, I guess. My wife never lets on to me if she wants to or not. The only way I can tell is if I start playing around with her, teasing her. If she teases back then I know it's all right. She can always tell if I want something. Things have changed pretty much since we first got married. For the first two or three months she didn't get any feeling out of it at all. Now she does almost every time I do.

"It's very important to me. It makes me feel like I enjoy living and that I love my wife and home and my kids. I guess if she weren't so afraid of getting pregnant I would want to more often, but she is so afraid and if I have to use rubbers I would just as soon not have it at all. The only way our relations could be better would be if she didn't have to worry and was more relaxed. I can always tell when she is afraid. She is tense and it is so much better when she is pregnant and don't worry about getting that way.

"Sex is important to her too, but she worries so much when she isn't pregnant that it's hard for her to enjoy it and relax. Then when she doesn't, she gets real nervous and nags at me all the time and the children too. But she isn't like that when she gets anything out of our relations. I guess I enjoy it the most, but that is because she isn't relaxed enough. I think it's just as important for her as it is for me. That's the reason I would like for her to enjoy it all of the time. I know she could if she didn't worry about pregnancy so much. That's why I am willing to do anything she thinks will help her."

Having too many children is for the Nelsons an inevitable outcome of the ways in which they live their life together. In the chapters that follow we will examine systematically various aspects of working class family life, and we will seek to show what helps or hinders effective family planning.

chapter iii

PATTERNS OF FAMILY PLANNING BEHAVIOR

> Every human society is faced with not one population problem but with two: how to beget and rear enough children and how not to beget and rear too many. *Margaret Mead, 1949*

THE CHOICE of whether or not to have a child is one which nature has made difficult for us. In the normal course of events men and women have children without any specific act on their part intended to produce this result. Our biology is such that the pleasures of sexual intercourse carry with them the likelihood of pregnancy, whether or not this be convenient for the persons involved. The species is thus perpetuated, many prospective parents are made happy, and quite a few other couples are made considerably less happy.

Human beings have at all times been preoccupied with their fertility—too much or too little—and have resorted to various magical, religious, and technological methods to achieve some control over the workings of their reproductive systems. Although man now has better means of control over parenthood than ever before, having children has not yet become fully a matter of choice rather than a purely natural occurrence. Our concern here will be with how effectively one group of Americans, the working class, is able to make use of what technology provides to limit and space their children.

Effective contraceptive action is made up of a series of separate, co-operative, and deliberate acts which involve both man and woman and which interfere with conception. Effective family planning involves a series of such acts properly performed over the wife's period of fecundity. The co-operative nature of contraceptive acts and the fact that they must be repeatedly performed if family limitation is to be achieved are of crucial importance in understanding couples' success or failure in carrying out their plans. These points are nicely illustrated in our data by those cases in which one party is strongly motivated for contraception and the other party does not co-operate.

> My husband and I don't talk too much [about family planning]. Sometimes he says we have too damn many and I say, "Yeah," and that is that. I told him Mom was taking me to the doctor and I don't know what he thought about it. I brought the diaphragm home and showed it to him. It didn't work; I think I'm pregnant now. I used it some of the time but not that one night. I went to bed early and by the time I was enough awake to know what was happening it was all over. I asked him to stop; I told him I didn't have my diaphragm on, but he acted like he couldn't hear. My husband tried rubbers but he says he's too big and they hurt him real bad. [Who should have the main responsibility for contraception?] The wife. She has to have the kids, so she won't forget. The husband should help, though, by not doing anything without asking the wife about whether she's got it in.

This lower-lower class woman already has more children than she wants—she has been married for four years and has three children spaced a year apart. She obviously wants no more and is willing to take as much responsibility for birth control as she can, but if her husband will not co-operate at the minimum level she requests, she cannot achieve her goal. Other women, perhaps more assertive, or perhaps with less impatient husbands, contend more successfully with the same issue:

> Well, I don't want a lot of kids, so I take care now not to get caught. I make my husband use something so I won't get

caught. I guess I was pretty dumb when I first got married but I'm not so dumb now. He uses a rubber; I don't let him stick it in me unless he has the rubber on. He likes it better with nothing on but I won't let him. Before we start doing it I make him get the rubber out of the drawer and I put it under the pillow, and then when he is ready to stick it in I give him the rubber and make him put it on. In the beginning he used to try to fool me and say he put it on when he didn't, but I can tell the difference and I caught him when he tried to pull it out like we used to do it, but I don't let him get away with that because that is the way I got caught the last time. [Whose should be the major responsibility?] Well, I made him get the rubbers. He likes it better without it; I think he is just in a hurry all the time and he is too lazy to put it on. In the beginning he didn't mind using it because he didn't want any more kids either, but every once in a while he tried to talk me out of it because on account of the time when he used to take it out my second kid was not born for a couple of years, so he says nothing will happen, that he will be careful. But I won't take any chances, so he knows that he can't do it to me unless he uses the rubber, so he doesn't argue so much any more.

This upper-lower class woman has been married for seven years and has a child of six and one of three. Effective contraception in her marriage is achieved against the constant grumbling of her husband, but it is effective because she is able to force him to co-operate. As might be expected, where co-operation fails, it is most often the husband who refuses participation in the contraceptive act.

The technology of contraception is deceptively simply; the total contraceptive act of which the method or appliance is only one part is complex, and in the dynamics of the required co-operative act there are many ways performance can fall short of that necessary for effectiveness. It seems likely that failures at the interpersonal level are more common than technical failures in the use of appliances. Our task in this chapter will be to examine in detail the series of acts that constitute effective contraceptive behavior and to seek the ways in which those couples who do not behave effectively fall short.

We will speak in the discussion which follows of two kinds of people, those who are effective at contraception and those who are not. These categorizations into effectives and non-effectives represent interpretations based on the interview data. By "effectives" we designate those respondents who, as best we could determine from our data, were using a contraceptive method properly and consistently at the time of the interview. By "non-effectives" we designate those respondents who seemed not to use a contraceptive method at all or who described their contraceptive practices in such a way as to suggest that they were using the method either improperly or sporadically. These categorizations are necessarily gross because they derive from an interpretation of self-descriptions by the respondents in our study; however, they will serve reasonably well for the purposes to which we wish to put them.

THE EXTENT OF FAMILY PLANNING AND LIMITATION PRACTICES

Family planning in Western civilization has a fairly recent origin (Lewinsohn, 1956). The movement grew up under the name of Neo-Malthusianism in the early nineteenth century as an answer to the dismal fate of over-population which Malthus and his followers predicted for the human race. This concern led to a revival of interest in contraceptive techniques, and by the end of the century the major methods used today had been advanced by various supporters; the condom, the pessary, suppositories, the rhythm method, douching, and withdrawal were all offered to the public with more or less publicity. Douching and withdrawal were probably the most widely used methods; even in the 1930's douching was the most common method used in the United States (Riley and White, 1940), and in England withdrawal is still the most common technique. While it is true that these methods left much to be desired in terms of technical efficacy, they did make it possible for couples to control the size of their families to a much greater extent than had been the case. In urban areas in particular, the middle classes and the more prosperous representatives of the working classes took up family planning with considerable interest. Families of two, three, or four children became the rule rather than the exception in these groups, and women were freed from the burden of being child-bearing machines.

The organized family planning movement has done much to foster the growth of contraceptive practices, perhaps mainly through its influence on professional groups. However, as with most other cultural acquisitions, the main impetus has come from individuals who reach out for the available techniques to solve their own intimate family problems without regard to the larger issues of population growth. Indeed, individual couples so address themselves to their own family planning without regard to these larger issues that the problem which disturbs the experts may at one time be underpopulation, at another time overpopulation.

During the 1930's population experts were concerned that the population of the United States might level off at about 160 million around the year 2000. At that time, it was feared that couples might control births so effectively that desirable population growth would not occur. The first large-scale study of the social psychology of family planning, organized to investigate factors in family planning and contraceptive behavior, grew out of this concern. This, the Indianapolis Fertility Study (Whelpton and Kiser, 1946), presented a thorough exploration both of family planning and contraceptive behavior in relation to various socio-economic factors and of the effect of such behavior on fertility.

A study conducted by Freedman, Whelpton, and Campbell (1959) during 1955 applies many of the Indianapolis Study methods to a national sample of 2,713 white married women in the child-bearing years. We will examine their findings in relation to factors of social status in family planning, since the quantitative data of that study will serve as a background to the qualitative approach used in our own research.

Goals and Expectations in Family Planning

Perhaps the central finding of the study is that, in the minds of most American women, the ideal number of children has shifted upward since the early 1940's. Almost half the women interviewed think the ideal American family should have at least four children. In 1941 only 26 per cent thought so. Similarly, in 1941 over 40 per cent of the women thought one or two children ideal, while in 1955 only 19 per cent thought so. It is also clear from the data that many women see the ideal American family as larger than the family they expect to have. Thus, while almost half the women interviewed said they would like a family of at least four children if they could begin their married life anew, only slightly over one-third said they actually wanted that many children in their present circumstances; economic pressures and sub-fecundity tend to make the individual goal lower than the cultural ideal.

Clearly, then, the American ideal is a three- or four-child family, and the family actually desired by women ranges from two to four. Few women want less than two, and few want more than four. Nowadays, two children make a small family, four make a good-sized family, and more than four is too large, so far as most women are concerned.

The authors note that the ideal and the expected family sizes have not nearly the rural-urban differences that might be expected; there is very little difference when one looks at younger wives in the two environments. Similarly, the ideal does not seem to vary greatly with social status; young women of all social classes seem to want about the same number of children. However, the actual births and the expectations of women who have been married a few years show a clear status difference. The lower the status (as measured most effectively in this study by the wife's education), the more children the respondents have, and the more they expect.

The patterns for Protestants and Catholics differ. For Protestants there is a clear-cut relationship to social class; the lower the status, the more children are expected. However, the differences between college-educated women, high school graduates, and women with only some high school education are relatively minor; it is the women with no more than grammar school education who show the higher fertility pattern.

Among Catholics, the pattern is more complex. At the time of the interview, they showed the same inverse relation between social class and number of births as the Protestant women. However, college-educated Catholic women hoped to have more children than any other group; grammar school women expected the next greatest number, and women with some high school education expected the least number. It seems, however, that younger Catholic women of higher status overestimate, in their enthusiasm for conformity with Church doctrine, since the experience of older Catholic women does not come close to the expectation (an average of four children) of these younger women. Apparently, large family goals eventually bow to the pressures of income and mothering.

It is clear that women of lower status have and expect to have more children than women of higher status. But the younger the woman, the more similarity there is between those of lower and higher status. Young lower class women obviously start with much the same aspirations as higher status women; over a period of time, however, they find themselves with more children than they thought they would have. How this comes about will be one of our main concerns in this study.

The Practice of Family Limitation

Given these goals and expectations, what do women at various status levels do about them? Specifically, what do they do to limit the number of children they have? Freedman and his colleagues discovered that the great majority of couples at all social levels sooner or later act to reduce the number of conceptions. They found that at least 80 per cent of couples in which the wife had at least some high school education do something designed to limit conception or plan to do so in the future; this is true of less than 60 per cent of women who have only a grammar school education. Their data also made clear a strong status difference in terms of when contraception is adopted. Among those who had ever used contraceptives, 68 per cent of the college women had adopted a contraceptive method before their first pregnancy, while only 24 per cent of the grammar school women had done so. Before their second pregnancy, 90 per cent of the college women had used a contraceptive, while only 29 per cent of the grammar school women had done so. By the time of their third pregnancy, only slightly more than half the grammar school women who subsequently used a contraceptive had done so, while over three-fourths of the women with more education had done so.

The Choice of Contraceptive Method

When it comes to particular contraceptive methods, the differences between status groups are clear-cut, though not so striking. Again, of course, religion makes a difference. Among Protestants, the so-called appliance methods (condom, diaphragm, douche, etc.) are most commonly used; 80 per cent of grammar school women and about 90 per cent of those with more education have used an appliance method at some time. The non-appliance methods (rhythm and withdrawal) are not exclusively used by a large proportion of any group: 20 per cent of the grammar school group and about 10 per cent of those with more education had used only such methods. Interestingly enough, among Catholics the rhythm system exclusively was used mostly by higher status women; 67 per cent of the college women and 52 per cent of the high school graduates had used only this method, compared to 34 per cent of the women with some high school education and 38 per cent of the grammar school women. Fewer Catholic women had tried any appliance method; the largest proportion was in the "some high school" group, where 60 per cent had used an appliance method, compared to 49 per cent of the grammar school group, 44 per cent of the high school graduates, and 31 per cent of the college women.

The two most widely used appliance methods, the condom and the diaphragm, also show status differences. These are most apparent among Protestants, since Catholics less often used these methods, and since the group who used them most heavily was the "some high school" group. (For example, among Catholics, 34 per cent of this group had used condoms, 29 per cent of the grammar school group, and only about 20 per cent of the women who had graduated from high school. The status differences for the diaphragm users were small, since only 17 per cent of the total group had ever used the method.)

Among Protestants, the condom had been used by 44 per cent of the grammar school group, by 46 per cent of those with some high school education, by 48 per cent of the high school graduates, and by 51 per cent of the college women. Obviously, the condom is fairly widely diffused. With the diaphragm, however, the story is quite different; 57 per cent of the college women had tried the method, 42 per cent of the high school graduates had also done so, 37 per cent of the women with some high school, and only 17 per cent of the grammar school women.

Success in Planning

We noted above that women of lower status have more children than women of higher status. This is due in part to the higher proportion of non-users of contraceptives in the lower status group; it is also due to the lesser effectiveness shown by lower status users. According to the study, by the time they reached the age period 30-34, 48 per cent of the fecund grammar school women who had ever used contraceptives had more children than they wished, while only 15 per cent or less of those with more education had been as unfortunate.

It is clear from this summary of the study by Freedman and his colleagues that the working class has the greatest problem with effective family planning, and that their difficulties arise at several levels: (1) they less often use contraception; (2) they adopt its use, if at all, at a later stage in their child-bearing histories; and (3) when they do use contraceptives, they are less likely to achieve their goals with them. It is also clear from the data that the most serious problem group in this connection is the group of lowest status; the differences among the subgroups who have attended at least high school are generally not as great as the differences between them and the grammar school group. This is particularly apparent in the number of children actually born.

Having had an overview of some of the behavioral aspects of family planning and limitation activities as they differ from one social class to another, we can now turn to an examination of some of the reasons for the patterns which Freedman, Whelpton, and Campbell find among those of lower status.

PATTERNS OF PLANNING AND LIMITATION

The family limitation behavior of working class couples is highly variegated; almost every couple shows an idiosyncratic way of doing something to prevent conception. However, we can outline four modal types which express the major tendencies present: (1) the early planners, (2) the "do nothing" group, (3) the sporadic users of contraceptives, and (4) the late, "desperate" limiters. The second and third groups do not behave in ways likely to result in effective contraception over any period of time. The first group is made up of couples who have carefully settled on some consistent family limitation system relatively early in their marriage. The fourth group consists of couples who have in desperation chosen contraception to put an end to having a greater number of children than they ever wanted.

The Early Planners

We have seen in the summary of the study by Freedman *et al* that working class women tend not to adopt contraception at all until after one or two pregnancies. This seems generally true of our own working class respondents. The group we call early planners, however, do adopt contraception before they have reached the desired family size. Often, they use contraception for spacing births after the first pregnancy. At other times, they experiment a bit so that there are one or two accidental pregnancies before they settle down in earnest with some effective method. In any case, they are distinguished from other groups by the fact that they have managed to be reasonably effective at contraception before they feel they must act in desperation.

For example, there is Mrs. Wallace, an upper-lower class woman who has been married for four years; she has a child two and a half years old and one of six weeks. She spoke of her family planning goals and techniques in this way:

> We both like four children. We've talked it over many times and are in perfect agreement that if we feel we can do for them financially as time goes on we'll have two more. I think four is ideal because there's more interest and congeniality in large families. We know we can't afford more than four, but that will be better than one or two. [Spacing?] The baby should arrive when the other child is two and a half years old. . . . I think the financial ability of the parents to support more children [is important in planning]. If you can't see your way clear to feed, clothe, and educate them on a good standard of living, then it's better not to have more children.
>
> We talked a lot about our family and our future; we knew before we were married about what we wanted. When Mary was a year old we began to talk of trying for another child; when she was fourteen months or a little more we said let's start trying now, so I didn't use the suppositories, and sure enough it wasn't long until I thought I was pregnant. [Why suppositories?] They were what my husband suggested I use when we were first married. They've been so successful for me that I doubt if I'll ever change to anything else; I've heard about the diaphragm, rubbers, withdrawal and jelly—if that's different from suppositories—but I haven't tried any of them. I didn't know anything about all of this before I was married; my husband explained all of it to me right before and on our wedding night. We had discussed about not having children right away. He bought the suppositories and told me how to use them right from the beginning of our married life.
>
> [Who should be responsible for contraception?] Definitely the wife. If she finds something that works for her, then she and her husband can both have this pleasure with no worries. If she doesn't feel safe she will be tense and not get the enjoyment out of it she should.

This couple obviously know what they want and have proceeded toward their goal in a highly organized manner. The openness Mrs. Wallace shows is perhaps one indication of the rationality with which the subject of planning is approached. It is also important that her husband is co-operative, and even the leader, in this activity. The Wallaces' effectiveness in planning seems closely related to the clarity of their goals—they want a large family, but they want to be certain that they can give their children the things an average American child should have. Therefore they have their children one at a time, spacing them for convenience but also to be sure that their financial resources can sustain them.

Planning from the beginning of marriage is not common among this group, as we have said. Even the relatively effective planners in the working class tend to start later. In a way, they seem to delay planning until they are sure they will have to plan. Mrs. Carlson is a good example of the more common pattern in the group which plans before they have had more children than they really want. A lower-lower class woman, she has been married for eight years and has children seven, six, and three years old:

> The three children I have are just what I want. My husband doesn't want any more either; we've talked about it. Three is all we can afford, that's all we can take care of sufficiently. If you can't give three enough, that's enough. I don't think it's important how they're spaced as long as one is walking and as long as your health is all right. Finances is the most important thing in deciding how many children, because if you can't support them that's bad.
> After the last baby was born I had such a hard time the doctor suggested I not have any more. So we've taken his advice about not having any more, but if I would become pregnant we would accept it. We use protection so I don't get pregnant. It is an understanding between us; it's been three years. I feel I don't want any more children. We use protection, just a rubber. I tell you frankly, I'd like a diaphragm but I'm just too embarrassed to go get one. They do very well; I have friends who use them and get very good results.
> I didn't know anything when I got married; everything I know I've learned since I got married. I learned that it [contraception] can be done because I've experienced it in the past three years. Actually it was six years because there's three years between the last two. I learned to use a douche bag and condoms. My husband doesn't mind using protection; as a matter of fact, he's all for it because it's protecting me—at least our doctor thinks it should be. [Who should be responsible for con-

traception?] Either one that it is most convenient for. I don't think it's up to the husband any more than the wife. After all, women get the satisfaction as much as the men and maybe you can't trust 'em. I'd sure hate to depend on the man entirely.

The Carlsons had two children immediately after their marriage and then began contraception. It is not clear whether the third child was an accident or not; in any case they were not too unhappy about it. However, their doctor's encouragement to limit their children to three obviously met with their agreement on financial as well as health grounds, and they are able to co-operate successfully with the technique that best fits their knowledge and Mrs. Carlson's modesty.

In this group of early planners, then, are those couples who either from the beginning of their marriages or through some process of experimenting have settled on a method with which they are content—or at least reasonably content, since there are also cases in which effectiveness in contraception is maintained against opposition by the husband, who is not as sensitive as the wife to the need for limitation.

The "Do-Nothing" Group

These are people who even after several years of marriage and several children make no effort to limit the number of children they have. They represent the opposite extreme from the early planners and are a similarly small group. Freedman, Whelpton, and Campbell (1959) showed that among older women (35-39) over 80 per cent of the fecund women had at one time or another done something contraceptively. In our data there are few couples with more than two or three children who have not tried a contraceptive method. Those in our sample who have had no experience with contraceptives after three children are almost all Catholics who have accepted large families as having positive value. Thus, one upper-lower class man who has four children (ages seven, five, four, and two) and who has been married for eight years said:

> I would like to have about five children. I think that is an ideal size; that is enough for a woman to look after. [Spacing?] Just as fast as you can have them. [What is important in deciding how many to have?] I think the mother's health—if she can bear them and care for them is the only thing. [Contraceptive practices?] We are Catholic and are not supposed to use any method but the rhythm method, which we do not even try to practice. I have used rubbers and pulling it out when I was single and running around but none since I was married. [What methods have you heard about?] The diaphragm and different greases and jellies, but I don't know anything about them. [Where did you learn?] I didn't know nothing much before I was married, only a layman's knowledge about how to use a rubber, which I learned from the fellows I ran around with. I learned about the rhythm method from the Church and the jellies and greases from talking to different people. [How does your wife feel about contraception?] My wife, like me, does not believe in it, as it would go against her religion.

Such a clear-cut insistence on doing nothing seems more characteristic of men than women. In our small sample, none of the fecund Catholic women with three or more children can be said to do nothing at all about contraception; they make some gesture in that direction, by douching or by trying the rhythm method at some time. Their attempts may not be very effective in limiting their families, but this is due to failures in execution rather than to a lack of desire. It seems likely that religious belief serves more to disorganize efforts at contraception than to prevent them completely. The ambivalence which a Catholic feels between adhering to the Church's proscription of appliance methods and doing something that seems more effective (or less trouble) than the rhythm method often makes it difficult for him to be consistent in contraceptive practices, but it does not generally prevent some experimentation with appliance methods.

More typical of the non-users are couples who do not

yet feel any sense of urgency about limiting the number of children they have. These are couples who have one or two or three children and are willing to have more; most of them will begin contraception at some time in the future. Often, they have given a fair amount of thought to contraceptive methods. For example, an upper-lower class woman with three children (ages three years, two years, and one month) who has been married for four years told the interviewer:

> We want six and we want them all at once. I don't want to be tied down with babies year after year. I want them to have the fun of growing up together, and I want us to be young enough parents to enjoy the family. We want one child every year for six years; that's enough to bring up well. Being young makes it easier; I want to be a young, happy mother, not old and still having children at 30. I like to dance and I want to have some fun, too. Did you ever see a young mother dancing with her teen-age sons? I have; it looks good, too. [Considerations?] Money and the kind of home you can give them is important. That you are well and peppy and feel like caring for them is another. All are reasons for having a family early and growing up with them. . . .
> We've talked it over and my husband wants six children, too. That's a nice round number and the size we can take care of. I think there has to be planning but it can be done. I went back to work after Debbie was born and worked until the second baby was past the eighth month. I had a woman who stayed here all day with them cheap. We could afford it, but I did not know Debbie very well and she got spoiled some, and I missed a lot. After the boy was born, I thought I would not go back to work but it was the same old trouble—money. Well, this time I know better. I'm going to stay with my children and let my husband have all of the fine feeling of supporting the family! We didn't seem to have enough money with two salaries, either; so we're going to do the best we can and get by with me at home this time. I know it was no good to leave the children and go to work, but now I'm going to really stay home and love them.
> [Did you know about limiting children before marriage?] I knew some of the usual things about spacing children to fit the budget and to fit into plans the husband and wife might have, but that was never a problem for us. Before we were married we talked that all out and we both found we were of the

same mind about having the right size family quick and growing up with them. I have not tried to space mine; it just happened there is 15 months between Debbie and Jimmy and 11 months between him and the baby. I had heard and read some things about birth control. I asked my doctor soon after marriage when I thought I might be pregnant and wasn't. I have learned there are several ways to limit or omit having babies but I am not interested in it and paid very little attention. My husband knew of nothing but condoms before we were married and I think he had used them before—I just think that, I don't know. Since marriage he has had no reason to be concerned. [Who should be responsible for contraception?] I think both the husband and wife should share the responsibility. They are the parents; they are the ones who will either enjoy the relationship or fight over it. Both are responsible.

[Contraceptive methods?] I know of all the various ones but I think the button is the best. The doctor fits it into the mouth of the tube and you have to go in to his office, not a hospital, to have yourself cleaned out. He removes the button, cleans the woman up, and replaces it. It is by far the best and safest way. This has to be done every three months and is a lot better than trying to get the diaphragm in at the right time. I don't mean that a diaphragm or a plain douche used quickly enough would not be safe, but if it were important that the wife did not conceive, a button is the best. The wife could be more natural, more spontaneous and never be afraid. I am glad that it is not a problem for me and it won't be for three more years. By the time I am 28 or even 30 I want my family here to enjoy life.

I use a douche now for cleanliness but if I were trying to be sure not to conceive the button would be the best for me and I would not hesitate to go and have one fitted. I am Catholic and I should not think this way, but you see too much in a neighborhood like this to think any other way. There are plenty of people who ought not to be allowed to have big families and then not take care of them. Religion is being forced to become more modern. I do not think the feeling about birth control is as hush-hush now as it was in my mother's day, or her mother's. I know this for a fact; my grandmother would not let her husband touch her for years and years. They had separate rooms since my mother was a little girl. Later it was a joke in the family, but it was very hush-hush stuff when she was growing up.

This woman deliberately does not use contraceptives and expects to use them when she has the number of children she wants. Her use and non-use are determined by her

family planning goals, and she will probably be as single-minded about using contraception as she is now about having children one after the other. Other non-users will undoubtedly have different experiences as they try to move from an unconcerned to a more organized approach to family planning.

The Sporadic or Careless Users

Most of the couples who have not been able to practice contraception effectively fall into this category—they have used contraceptives, often several different kinds, but they are not able to use them in any satisfactory and consistent way. For example, one lower-lower class mother of five (ages fourteen, twelve, nine, five, and two) told the interviewer:

> I wanted four children, but I got five and am expecting another in about a month. My husband and I never discussed how many children we would have. Five was an ideal family to me; this is going to be one too many. I think children should be spaced three years apart, because that will give you a chance to have the one trained and broke pretty much.
> We use rubbers most of the time. I have no objection to them; my husband doesn't either. The only thing is, when we don't have them and we take a chance. We tried the diaphragm but it was too much trouble and I was afraid to use it anyway. We don't talk much about it; I would rather he just didn't do it at all. We tried the rhythm system; that's why I'm pregnant now, it didn't work. I've used a douche with Lysol but I didn't trust that either. He tried just pulling it out [withdrawal] but he said he couldn't do that. [When did you learn about these things?] All of these ways I've learned since I was married, from friends and books I've read on married life. [How does your husband feel about contraception?] His ideas are just that when he wants something he wants it and let things happen as they will. I guess he feels that way because he thinks that is what a wife is for, to satisfy her husband's desires. [Who should be responsible for contraception?] I think the man should because he knows when he is reaching a climax and I don't, and he's the one who's getting the good out of it, not me.

This woman wants to limit the size of her family and, from what she says, her husband also wishes they did not have so many children. However, these desires do not lead to effective action. Instead, their motivation seems to have resulted mainly in switching from one method to another in the hope that something would turn up that is feasible, given their particular frictions and disagreements over sexual relations. Since no such method exists and since this woman seems to reject sexuality so completely that she cannot even protect herself contraceptively, they have more children than they want, and they are inclined to blame the methods rather than themselves.

Another lower-lower class woman with five children tells a similar story, although she has not been so energetic in trying various methods:

> Sometimes we, my husband that is, uses rubbers. I planned on two kids but as you can see my plans didn't work out. The difficulties are my husband says he has a rubber on and don't, and bang, I'm knocked up! Sometimes I wash myself or take a hot bath. [What did you know about contraception?] I had sex only once before I was married. All the rest I learned from my mother and husband. I guess I still don't know too much. [What does your husband think about contraception?] He thinks they cost too much money and would rather spend it on beer. My husband was a boxer for a while and he is quite strong, so I don't argue with him too much. We never discuss sex; we do it when we feel like it.

This woman feels victimized by her husband but is too passive to do anything about his untrustworthiness. She fears him too much to insist that he use condoms, and (later in the interview) she says that she is equally afraid of a diaphragm. She reconciles herself to recurrent pregnancies.

Often, the desperation these women feel leads them to think of sterilization as the only way out; when they have tried several methods with poor results and discarded others as too much trouble or too messy, "having my tubes tied" seems the last possible refuge against continuing to be a child-bearing machine. Thus, a lower-lower class woman with five children (ages seven, six, five, three, and one) told us:

> I wanted only two, a boy and a girl, and I wanted to do right for them. I wanted to be naturally happy and glad about my family. My mother was an awful mother. She had a hard time and took it out on us kids. After all, when you have five or six kids what good is a woman then, to the kids or the husband. She is tired out and, and, and [can't finish the thought]. It's hard on her; she's a mess. Any woman would be, and that is what's happening to me and I'm not going on this way.
>
> [Have you and your husband talked about limitation?] Sure, we talked it over, but what good is that going to do if you are all the time getting pregnant? You're never safe when you're in good health, and that's one thing, my husband is very healthy and I am ready at any time. We tried rubbers but it is not safe —the only thing is for me to really take care of myself before I come home from the hospital this time. I'm going to do something and no one is talking me out of it because I do not intend for my family to know anything about it until afterwards. If my doctor will not tie me up for a couple of years then I will get a diaphragm, but before I come home and run into any more trouble. I want to be able to enjoy the children I have now and not be tied to this house until I never have any kind of life for myself.
>
> [What methods do you use?] That's the trouble, we don't use anything. I think my husband is going to put on a rubber and he don't half the time. And I can't depend on rhythm; I think it's all right and half the time it isn't. I have heard about all the different methods but for me I know I ought to be tied and have it over for a while. You know, it doesn't have to be permanent; they can tie you for a couple of years, time enough for you to get your breath. I'm always having a baby, getting over having a baby, or having kidney trouble. I'm tired of it.
>
> [What have you learned about contraception?] It's my husband that never heard about it. He is the one that is careless and goes in for too much fooling around. He doesn't have all the work and trouble, sure it's all fun for him! He likes the kids and likes the idea of a big family, but he doesn't take care of the kids; I have to all the time. When I was first married I thought getting furniture and keeping house was going to be a lot of fun. From the very start I was pregnant! I've heard a lot [about contraception], mostly from women talking. At the clinic you have to sit and wait and you get to talking. We are

all in the same boat and we have a lot to talk about, especially when you see the same people there year after year. They almost always come back sometime when you are there again. They tell all their experiences; I learned a lot that way. I knew something about contraception before we were married but I am Catholic and I believed we would be all right with rhythm, but it did not take long to find out how that will not work for us!

[How does your husband feel?] He thinks that we ought to do something now. This time for sure, as it is not right to go on this way with a baby every year and no life of our own. He is willing but I have not talked too much to him about it. I know he will not wear a rubber if he can get out of it so it will be up to me, and I sure intend to protect myself this time. [Who should be responsible?] I think the man is but I know it does not work that way, so I guess it is up to the wife. She is the one who has the trouble and the pain, not the man. I am convinced that the real safe way is to be tied and I am going to have my doctor do the job. I am not going to say anything to the priest. Who is he to tell me about how many children to have? He never has to drag about with five kids and try to make a living for them! The way things are it just goes on making me old and cross and sick!

The interview provided this woman with an opportunity for a tirade against her husband, the priest, and her fate in general. Her desperation is eloquently told. Her inner resources do not allow her to control the circumstances of sexual relations in such a way that she could be effective with the two contraceptive methods she and her husband have tried; she is willing to solve the problem once and for all by sterilization. If her doctor refuses she will take the responsibility herself and use a diaphragm, although she is unsure about her ability to make it work.

It is interesting that the men in our sample who fit this category of ineffective users do not show the same desperation. It is their wives who perceive the problem most keenly and worry most about it, but they cannot discuss the matter freely with their husbands, both because of their own reticence and because of the husband's unwillingness to concern himself. The husbands do not tell us that they try to trick their wives when they use a condom; instead, they tend to blame fate for their troubles or to say that one should have as many children as God wills. At the same time, they often would prefer to have no more children and are quite happy if the wife goes to the trouble of doing something to prevent conception so long as what is done does not interfere with their pleasure in sexual relations. Their preferences about family limitation are often reasonably clear but do not operate successfully and regularly at the times when they must if conception is to be prevented.

The examples given above seem typical of the 50 per cent of fecund grammar school women who by the time they are 34 have had more children than they want, despite some use of contraception. The woman quoted last is doing her best to move in the direction of effective contraception. Her story is typical of the group we take up next, and her experiences commonly precede a desperate loyalty to some effective way of guaranteeing that one will have no more children.

The Late, "Desperate" Limiters

These are couples who begin the consistent use of contraceptives after they have had as many children as they want. During their ineffective period they have experimented with several methods, and they often seek to amuse the interviewer by naming each child by the method which failed in his case—this one is a "rhythm baby," that one a "douche baby," etc. Finally they settle on a method that somehow works for them; the method may be one new to them or one discarded earlier and returned to later with greater care. In any case, they have been schooled in contraception by adversity and defeat and have learned their lesson well. They often show a dogged determination which the early planners do not because they do not feel as pressed—"I make my husband use those whatchamacallums, those rubbers. I wouldn't let him come near me if he didn't use them. I make my man use rubbers, I sure do!"

An upper-lower class mother of five (ages seven, six, five, four, and eight months) told this story:

> These five children are enough for any young couple, unless you are out on a farm. Three's my ideal, but I got lost somewhere along the way. It's a problem when you are in an apartment. They are very good about the house but it's this outside business that gets me down. In the beginning I didn't use any [contraception] at all; just as they came, they came. But now it's the education of the future to worry about. It's not just having two bedrooms, we have to think about five bedrooms and two bathrooms. A big family is a big expense. You can't pass clothes down like they say; they're all worn out by the time the next one is ready for them.
>
> You definitely have to use something if you're like me; I never used any before but I got pregnant so easy I have to now. I tried to work it certain times of the month but I became pregnant anyway. Now I use the diaphragm but the doctor says nothing is really safe. For me there's no safe days [laughs]. We used the prophylactics, too, but I like the diaphragm. I think the woman should use what is necessary. After our fourth child the doctor told me about the fertile times in a woman's body —that's how our fifth one was born; there's no not-fertile time for me [laughing, then serious again]. I can get pregnant it seems to me every time. Now I use the diaphragm.
>
> [How about your husband?] I just think any normal man wishes that he didn't have to use anything, but they have to expect it if they make up their minds that that's it. We talked about getting the diaphragm. He seemed to be more interested about how I would react than about himself. We both accept it and don't discuss it too much. He knows how I am and that I am the type of person that gets pregnant so some precautions have to be taken or we will keep increasing our family. [What about condoms?] I can't help but feel that 75 per cent of sex is for the man, so I feel it should be the woman that has to.

This woman understands contraception; she is anxious to use her knowledge effectively and she has co-operation from her husband. Together, they are able to look forward to having no more children so that they may give what they want to the ones they have.

A lower-lower class man with four children (ages eleven, five, five, and three) tells a similar story:

> I wanted two and my wife wanted one. After we had four we talked about it and she said she didn't want any more. I think two, a boy and a girl, is an ideal size. I just don't believe in people having five or six and not giving them the things they need and should have. We talked about not having any more. I use rubbers, they're the only thing I like to use. We've used the calendar way and her getting up and cleaning herself out. That withdrawal don't work; I tried it and that's how the last one come. The calendar ain't no good either. All year it changes; it could be the first part of the month or the last, you can't go by it. [Who should be responsible?] The man, I think he knows what he can do and what he can't do; what he can support and what he can't.

This man is quite willing to take responsibility for contraception; he feels it is in his own interest, since he is quite concerned about his ability to support more children. His experimentation with what seemed an easier method (withdrawal) led to the last unwanted pregnancy; now he consistently uses a method which he feels sure will work.

Another lower-lower class man, also the father of four children, has an added reason for not having more children:

> We have talked it over several times and decided to be careful to keep her from getting knocked up, or pregnant as you say. It's the only thing for us as the doctor said my wife must not have any more children. We use special strong rubbers which I order from a druggist. We must be sure and I think this is best. We have tried the jelly you use by itself but we were afraid it would not be safe. [How does your wife feel about contraception?] My wife feels about the same way as I do, and she knows we must practice birth control as having a baby would be pretty apt to kill her. She knows a man must have intercourse to be happy if he is strong and healthy, so she tries to please me. [Who should be responsible?] I think the man should have the main responsibility as a woman cannot get pregnant without a man around, and it is easier for a man to use some protection than it is for a woman.

For these men and women, contraception has become a very meaningful and serious business. Through a process of trial-and-error they have settled on a method which they "swear by" (while "swearing at" the methods that failed them), and they use it consistently. The couples in this category of late, desperate users are often quite similar to those in the sporadic or careless group. Experience has made a strong impression on them, however, and often an authoritative or sympathetic physician has been able to help them work toward some rational way of dealing with the problem of family size.

Generally, then, our data suggest four patterns of family limitation activity: two kinds of effective and two kinds of ineffective contraceptive users. The early planners represent the ideal offered by those who advocate planning a family; they start planning relatively early in their child-bearing history and practice contraception effectively. The late, desperate users reach the same point only after having had all the children they feel they should have—after reaching the breaking point in the family budget or the wife's health. The non-users, few in number, use nothing even though they have no special desire for more children. The sporadic or careless users, who represent the bulk of those who constitute a problem in family planning and limitation, are couples with some desire to limit their families but who for a variety of reasons are unable to practice contraception effectively even though they may have considerable knowledge about various methods. In the chapters that follow we will discuss some of the psychosocial factors which lie behind these patterns, and show how they come about and how they fit the style of life and the personalities of the couples involved.

chapter iv

ASSUMPTIONS AND ORIENTATIONS IN FAMILY PLANNING

HAVING EXAMINED various patterns of contraceptive action among working class couples, we can turn to the goals, assumptions, and orientations to the world which these couples reveal in their family planning. Their reasons for planning have much to do with the way they act to achieve their plans. The attitudes and conceptions with which these people approach family planning and limitation have much to do with their success in being consistent and co-operative about contraception. Their ideas about themselves as effective agents in their own destinies strongly affect both the energy they bring to bear on this problem and the degree to which they try to put their family life goals into practice.

Almost all the working class men and women we interviewed have some more or less specific idea of how many children they want. Most of these couples have given some thought to what would be a desirable family size and have some feeling about how many children would be too many, how many would be too few. But the amount of thought different people give to this issue varies widely. It appears that women think more about family size than men—as one would expect, since it is the woman who bears the major responsibility for keeping the home running. Also, some couples have obviously discussed their family's size a great deal, while others have talked about it only in fits and starts, with no concensus developed to guide their actions.

RATIONALES IN FAMILY PLANNING

Two major reasons for limiting a family are given by most of our respondents: the necessity to support the children one has, and consideration of the wife's health. A third issue, not often mentioned, is the more interpersonal one of the effect of the number of children on relationships within the family.

"You Shouldn't Have More Than You Can Support"

The most common and clear-cut rationale for limiting the number of children one has is financial. Two versions of the economic argument are apparent. In one, the emphasis is on bare necessities, on feeding the mouths for which one has made oneself responsible. The working class respondents who are most absorbed with these concerns tend to come from the lower-lower portion of the group. Their anxiety about having more children than they want springs from worry about providing the minimum necessities for the children (and for the parents, since more children mean less to go around). A lower-lower class man who moved to Cincinnati from the Kentucky hills commented:

> I think planning a family is the only thing in the cities at the present time. Large families grew up on the farm and did all right as they always had plenty of food. Here a man has to struggle to feed anything of a family.

And a lower-lower class woman with five children who is desperately hopeful that douching will keep her from getting pregnant again told the interviewer:

> We can't feed what we got now. I think it's how much money you got that decides you on how many kids you should have.

> I'm sick of it now and don't want any more. I think I have the ideal family.

Such concern with bare subsistence does not generally seem to result in effective family limitation, for reasons that will be discussed later. Among couples who think mainly in these terms, family planning has a strong connotation of coercion and artificiality; the motivation is heavily negative and is oriented toward avoiding starvation (in fantasy, if not, thanks to welfare measures, in actuality). The man or woman who talks about limitation as necessary because life in the city is meager compared to the rural cornucopia is saying in effect, "We are trying to limit how many children we have not because we want to but because we must; we do it because of the horrible consequences of not doing so, not because we gain something positive."

The other way of phrasing an economic concern has more to do with the positive gains of income above the subsistence level. Here emphasis is on the relationship between number of children and ability to secure better things for the family. This is not a question of how many mouths one can feed but how well one can feed them, how well one can clothe and educate and entertain oneself and one's children. The economic argument often serves as a symbol of one's ability to maintain a respectable and socially desirable environment for children and to give them various advantages. Thus, one lower-lower class man whose wife was pregnant with their first child chose a concrete illustration of such advantages:

> I want two children and no more. My wife agrees that two or three are ideal. I think there are three main things to consider: first, make enough money to support them, next, for the mother to like them and like to raise them, and last, a place with a fenced-in yard for them to play in so they can grow up right, not running in the streets.

The contrast between a person's own childhood and what he wants for his children is frequently used to good effect. Working class parents whose own parents had a hard time rearing their children may try conscientiously to do better, to strive for higher standards of living than they themselves grew up with. This is perhaps most keenly felt by the fathers, who pride themselves on doing better than their own fathers, but their wives usually feel relieved when their husbands have such aspirations.

To the extent that a financial rationale for family limitation moves away from a concern with bare subsistence, it describes a particular way of life with particular standards that require a certain income to maintain. Where such goals are strongly held, the couple is more likely to give serious attention to family planning and limitation. However, as shown below, such an orientation requires considerable security about one's future.

Financial reasons for limiting the number of children carry strong moral authority. One is supposed to be responsible toward children, to care for them to the best of one's ability and to see to it that they have at least a minimum of mothering and respectability. Catholics are most likely to use economic reasons in arguing against what they believe their Church tells them. They usually know that the Church allows the rhythm method of contraception, but many believe that the method does not work. When they use an appliance, they are likely to justify it on the grounds that they must do so if they are to do right by their children; they say that the Church has no right to demand their exposure to the risk of too many children. Thus one upper-lower class woman, whose husband uses condoms to limit their family to three children, said:

> My husband is a strict Catholic, but he wants to be a good father to the ones he got. He even told the priest that. He said he'd have as many kids as the priest wanted if the priest sent him a check every month. The priest had a fit. We both confess it and have to make a penance for it.

Hostility is often directed toward the priest in this way: "I'll have them if you and the Church want to support them."

"The Mother's Health Shouldn't Be Endangered"

Generally coupled with monetary reasons for limiting family size is a concern about the wife's health. For men this is often a mysterious but powerful inhibitor of the tendency to have more children. For women it is often a way of justifying their unwillingness to bear children year in and year out. Health reasons apply particularly to concerns about spacing children and to having more than five. On the latter score, women often express concern about being old before their time if they have too many children. Men are obviously impressed by the dramatic changes which take place with pregnancy and delivery, and their wives often use excuses related to "female trouble" to avoid sexual relations as well as to limit the number of children they have. It is not surprising, then, that men show considerable anxiety about what pregnancy may do to their wives, although this anxiety does not often cause them to do anything effective about contraception. One twenty-four-year-old lower-lower class man with three children who sporadically practices rhythm told the interviewer:

> Well, a family's size should depend on a woman's health and a lot of things. You have to go on the condition of health. If she has too many babies too close together, it will kill her.

In particular cases, health may be more directly a reason for limiting the number of children to less than four or five. A woman who believes that for some reason she should not have more children may persuade her husband of this. It is difficult to tell from our data to what extent this results from medically-diagnosed conditions and to what extent from the woman's own wishfulness, her desire to justify not having more children by saying that it would be bad for her physically.

"You Shouldn't Have Them If You Don't Want Them"

Health and finances are the most acceptable reasons for limiting children in the working class. Much less often, more personal reasons are given. While from the point of view of mental hygiene it is true that a wanted child is more likely to be a healthy child, many working class women find it difficult to admit that they simply do not want more children, that they would find another child a burden rather than a pleasure. The more children the woman has, the more likely she is to face up to this fact and to realize that having more children is good neither for her nor for the youngsters. One thirty-four-year-old lower-lower class woman, pregnant with an unwanted fourth child, commented:

> I think the amount of children you want is important. I don't think anyone should have more than they really want because they feel kind of hard toward the babies, I think, and that's not fair to them.

Another lower-lower class woman, younger and more effective in her contraceptive practices, perceives this, too:

> I'd say two children [she has two] would be ideal, about two years apart. Your feelings toward children are the most important thing in deciding how many to have, and then your income. You should be able to give them everything; they are your responsibility.

It seems likely that some such admission is necessary for effective limitation; if the couple cannot admit to themselves that they really don't want another child, it is unlikely that they will be able to maintain the co-operative action necessary for effective contraception. Wanting or not wanting a child is a more personal phrasing of the objective rationales so easy to give; this kind of personal phrasing, this acceptance of the relevance to "us" of the more objective rationales, is perhaps at the core of concerted planning.

FAMILY PLANNING AS AN EGO FUNCTION

In order to accomplish the goals established with the rationales discussed above, it is necessary to act according to a plan. It should be clear from our examination of the various patterns of family planning and limitation that we are dealing with a complex area in which several forces are at play. A number of different and sometimes conflicting needs and values must be brought into some kind of integration which permits the consistent, co-operative behavior necessary for effective contraception. Such an integration of varying forces is a function of the individual's ego, his organizing and executive capacities. It will be helpful if before we begin our examination of the separate conditioning factors in the following chapters, we pause first to concern ourselves directly with some of the characteristics of planning and making choices as they operate in connection with family planning as an activity of the ego.

Planning and the Problem of Choice

The ideas of family planning and planned parenthood embody a particular world view, a particular way of looking at the world and at oneself. Planning to become a parent implies that the planner is an adult member of society who makes a choice and who accepts the responsibility which that choice entails. This kind of planning suggests conscious thought and intention related to the alternatives of parenthood and nonparenthood, and it implies that the individual considers the two alternatives available to him as voluntary, neither of them inevitable or beyond his control.

Planning means that one looks ahead, orients himself toward the future, and commits himself and others to some course of action. Middle class people are used to doing this, and the ramified consequences of looking ahead and making commitments characterize the middle class way of life in connection not only with the family but also with the worlds of work, education, voluntary associations, and the like. Middle class people live in a matrix of commitments toward the future—both for themselves in terms of personal goals, and to other people in terms of reasonably clear-cut obligations. Planning thus involves a picture of the way things will be in the future and of the way one will be and act then. It requires the ability to project oneself at a present moment into a future one, to imagine how that future will be and how one can act in it. If for some reason one does not have the ability thus to project, it is not possible to plan in any effective manner. Many observers have commented on the elaborate training which middle class people have in just this kind of planning for the future, and on the relative lack of training which working class children are given in such methods of coping with life (Davis, 1948).

Two relevant conditions for the success of any planning need to be considered here; many interferences with effective family planning discussed in the following chapters have to do with one or the other. First, an orientation to the future, an ability to look ahead, implies that one has some feeling of trust about the future, that one feels the future is in relevant ways reasonably predictable. Implicit in every plan is a belief in a more or less stable world; if one cannot assume a stable, predictable world, it is very difficult to plan, since one cannot confidently imagine the conditions being planned for.

This kind of basic trust in the future is an important ingredient in that over-all personal stability of which planning is a part, as many writers on ego psychology have noted (French, 1952; Erikson, 1956). Where such a condition is lacking, behavior tends to be oriented toward present interests and pleasures; the individual finds it difficult to postpone pleasure in hope of some future gain, and has difficulty imagining himself as a person who has continuity and consistency. French has made a sense of trust about the future a central element in his theory of the ego's capacity to integrate man's needs with reality; he notes that hope of satisfaction activates the guiding influence of a plan and that the ability to plan varies directly with one's confidence of attaining his goal.

A sense of stability about and trust in the future, then, is one precondition for consistent planning. Closely related to this is a belief that one can affect one's future, can determine to some extent what will happen. This, too, is part of one's hope about the future. In addition to assuming certain things about what the world around him will be like, a person has to be able to assume that he can be effectively assertive in that world, that he can mold the future closer to his heart's desire. In fantasy this may be done by wishfulness, but in the real world one must be able to act in specific ways, and acting in these ways requires a certain confidence in one's ability both to control oneself and to be partly in control of the outside world.

Various studies of lower class people indicate that much in their upbringing and in their conditions of life makes it difficult for them to feel deeply these two requisites for planning. Our studies of working class adolescents (Rainwater, 1956) and housewives (Rainwater, Coleman, and Handel, 1959) suggest that, compared to middle class people, trust in a predictable and reasonably gratifying future is not common, nor is a belief in one's personal efficacy in relation to that future. Working class people tend to have a basic belief that what happens in the world is determined mainly by external forces against which their own energies are not likely to be effective. They are anxious over what they see as a depriving world, one which is also chaotic and unpredictable, governed by forces not easily understood. They are uncertain about the future; they accept things as given and pour little energy into either self-exploration or exploration of the outer world. They tend to view thinking negatively, to regard thought and planning as painful activities to be engaged in only under the pressure of great necessity. Even then, they are not optimistic, since they often feel that the best they can do will not be sufficient to overcome adversity—one may be spared unpleasantness by good fortune, one may be "lucky," but one cannot be personally successful against difficulty. Such a world view and way of thinking about oneself in the world are not conducive to effective planning. Indeed, they tend to discourage planning and the hope it implies, lest one court disappointment.

Naturalness and Artificiality in the Planning Process

When the event to be planned is as significant as parenthood, the dynamics of the choice are likely to become even more muddled, particularly since what one is planning is not really parenthood at all, but nonparenthood. One who exercises the choice to do nothing at all, to plan only in the negative sense, is quite likely to become a parent. Only if a person takes positive action and does something that is not spontaneous is parenthood avoided. The planning that is relevant to contraception is oriented toward *not being* a parent; if a couple is fecund, planning *to be* a parent requires only that they leave nature alone, doing nothing that is not spontaneous or instinctive in any case.

People thus tend to consider *not* planning as the natural way of doing things and planning as an artificial way of behaving. This is probably as true of middle class as of lower class people. "Doing what comes naturally" in connection with having children means not to concern oneself about spacing, limitation, or contraception. To take positive steps in this direction means to most people that they do something artificial in the most specific sense of the word (that is, "brought into being not by nature but by art or effort"). The artificial quality of family planning is heightened because planning involves in one way or another an interference in the spontaneous sequence of sexual activity. All the contraceptive methods in use today require some kind of interruption of this sequence, and in the contraceptive habits of most middle and lower class couples the interruption is closely connected with the sexual act—the contraceptive decision is made after the preliminaries to intercourse are in progress.

At a less concrete level, too, family planning tends to be regarded as unnatural, especially by lower class people. There is a general feeling that one really ought to be governed by nature, that one should have as many children as God wills. Realistic considerations may prevent this, but in limiting the number of children one feels forced to act artificially. Often the fault is laid to the conditions of modern urban life—on the farm it would not be necessary to limit the family to three or four children. Many working class men and women feel strongly that the number of children they have and the timing between them should be left "in the hands of Mother Nature." In a proper world one would allow nature to dictate these matters, would go along with nature's plan rather than make a plan of one's own: "I wish I could have all the children God would give me, but I know I can't afford them." As is apparent in this lower-lower class man's remark, family limitation is often looked upon as depriving one of the large family nature would like to give; one must deprive oneself because one cannot afford the expense of having the large family he might naturally have.

The naturalness of a larger family than he can afford is often reinforced by the lower class person's childhood experiences. Many lower class people grew up in large families. Often, despite the hardships they experienced, they think of their families with a great deal of affection and wish they could duplicate them in their own marriages. It is possible that some lower class couples who end up with more children than they want are unconsciously emulating their parents despite their more conscious desires to have a family size more in keeping with their financial resources for urban living.

The naturalness of having many children and the artificiality of having few is neatly illustrated by our respondents' comments when we asked them to describe the kind of person who would want only one child and the kind who would want seven children. Although both desires seem extreme to most working class people, the woman who wants seven is generally treated much more positively:

> [Seven children] She would probably be wealthy, kindhearted to want so many. A very sweet person and other people would probably like her very much.
> [One child] Very selfish, or very sick. Probably selfish. Not wanting to be tied down, very self-centered.
> [Seven children] She must love children a lot.
> [One child] It's not fair. It's self-centered. She wants no responsibility.

Even when the woman who wants seven children is condemned, it is on the basis that she is somehow unrealistic, that she overestimates her own or her husband's resources, and not because there is anything inherently unnatural in her desire. The woman who wants only one child is condemned much more emphatically for being a bad person, for going against her nature—and the woman who wants no children is beyond the pale, she should not have married at all.

In summary, then, there are two levels at which family planning activities are regarded as unnatural and artificial. First, contraceptive practice represents an interruption of spontaneous sexual relations: one does something artificial to avoid the consequences of "natural" sexual intercourse. (And it should be noted that such "natural" methods as the rhythm system often seem artificial to our respondents because they require abstinence at certain times when one would not "naturally" abstain.) Second, the reason for contraception, limiting and spacing children, is in itself regarded as unnatural. Most working class people have a deep, not consciously formulated belief that nature "wants" people to have many children and that when they limit the number of children they go against nature, although doing so may be legitimate in terms of the realities of life. It seems likely that these considerations are at the basis of many couples' religious feelings about contraception; such feelings may be codified and developed by a church, as in the case of Catholic doctrine, or they may exist as more vaguely formulated religious sentiments, as is the case with many of working class Protestant couples who feel that they must have good reasons for limiting their families if they are to feel moral about doing so.

The deeply held and often unconscious beliefs which many of our respondents have about the unnaturalness of "birth control" often interfere with the ways in which they carry out their family planning goals. Their feelings about contraception itself represent a kind of "tactical" resistance to effective planning; those about the unnaturalness of conscious planning represent a more strategic resistance, and one which probably plays a large role in making many working class couples so ineffective in contraceptive techniques.

Fantasied Birth Control: Wishfulness and the Role of Fate

We have noted the complexity of the family planning process and its relation to deeply held beliefs about what is natural and unnatural for a man and woman who live together as husband and wife. We have seen earlier that many working class couples do not manage to sustain the complex behavior and self-control necessary for effective family planning. One central theme which runs through ineffective couples' thinking about contraception has to do with a kind of wishfulness and a belief in fate and chance as important elements in the realization of family planning goals.

Fundamentally, such people are passive toward what they see as the externally operating forces of fate and chance. They believe that what they themselves do is only part of an over-all pattern of life by which what actually happens is determined. One is not master of one's fate. The simplest kind of belief in luck is reflected in statements like this from a twenty-one-year-old lower-lower class woman with two children:

> We thought about maybe three or four children would be nice; that's ideal I would say. [What do you do about it?] We don't use anything; we just trust to luck.

The feeling shown here is that what will be will be, that family size is determined by the immanent force of nature or God, and that one can hope and wish for three or four children but one does not have any really active role in determining what actually happens. In general, women seem less susceptible to such passive acceptance of fate than are men. While some women who have not yet had the three or four children they are willing to have express these sentiments, they find themselves hard-pressed to maintain such passivity when they have more. Men, in contrast, seem to hold to such ideas longer, and the result is often conflict between husband and wife.

For such people, sexual intercourse often seems to be a gamble—the result may or may not be children, depending on what fate decrees. Behind the easy acceptance that some men try to maintain often lie deep feelings of inadequacy to do anything about what may happen. Passive acceptance becomes a way of dealing with one's inadequacy and uncertainty. The man in essence says to his wife, "Don't embarrass me by asking me to do something to stop the children from coming; I'm not sure I can, so just shut up and accept things the way they are."

The individual may take a more active role and try to manipulate fate in some way. He still believes that chance plays a big role, but he is willing to help a bit, to gamble a little more positively. Such an attitude seems common among the sporadic or careless contraceptive users. The contraceptive in these cases seems to be a kind of magical talisman, a way of helping benevolent fate. But in such an attitude there is not much confidence in the method—it may not be powerful enough to stave off one's ultimate destiny; sooner or later luck will run out.

"Luck" is commonly referred to in discussions of contraception with people of this type; respondents often refer to being unlucky with a particular method. The phrasing they use indicates that they are more imbued with the idea that a magical force stepped in to frustrate them than with some more rational understanding of technical failure. When they are unlucky with one method, they seek another; the result is that many of these people move from one method to another through a series of pregnancies until they find one which they can settle down with on a more instrumental, less magical basis. It is understandable that the most widely accepted method, the condom, is also the one that is most easily understood, the one that seems the least mysterious and least magical.

The constellation of beliefs represented by such ideas as "luck," "taking a chance," and "being caught" points to another aspect of fantasied birth control. Many ineffective users behave as if using a contraceptive were important mainly as an indication of good intention—they are "good" about contraception and therefore deserve to be treated kindly by fate. They act as if an occasional lapse in use may be "forgiven" by fate, almost as if conception were an additive phenomenon; if one is "good" most of the time, a few lapses will be ignored. Again, such attitudes are probably more deeply held by men than by women, the latter being forced to a more rational appreciation of the matter.

It is interesting that women have a more developed vocabulary in this area than men. Such terms as "protection" and "birth control" seem more commonly used by women and seem to be more meaningful to them. The woman seeks to protect herself from the consequences of intercourse and very much wants that "protection"; she is often ready to criticize her husband for not understanding its importance and for his indifference to the suffering that lack of protection may cause her. When the words "birth control" are used, they usually come from a person with an organized conception of family planning, one whose contraceptive action is oriented to a fairly long time span and is incorporated into a plan rather than directed toward "on-the-spot" protection. "Protection" suggests at least a minimum of personally integrated contraceptive action and some departure from reliance on good luck; "birth control" symbolizes a further step in the direction of meaningful planning.

For many working class people, particularly those in the lower-lower class, family planning represents a confusing problem, one with which they feel ill-equipped to deal, and one which is simply another facet of a world seen as chaotic, difficult to understand, and very difficult to master in a personally effective way. For such people, their response is often one of wishfulness, of hoping that luck will hold and that children will be happily spaced, evenly distributed as to sex, and limited to a manageable number. Couples with these views often make token efforts to help fate, to improve their chances, but they do so in a context of uncertainty which gives them little confidence in their efforts and which therefore lessens their vigor in contraceptive practice. As in so many other areas of their lives, wishfulness is substituted for action; family size is a subject for fantasy and tentative goals, but not one to which concerted effort is devoted.

chapter v

SOCIAL ROLE AND SELF-CONCEPT IN THE MARITAL RELATIONSHIP

Family planning goals and behavior are intimately related to the ways in which working class husbands and wives see themselves in marriage and to the roles which they come to play as marital relationships develop. Several aspects of marital and family relationships are important here. At its inception, how do working class men and women think about the family they are about to found? How do they define the functions which a good husband and a good wife must perform in the family? How do they think of themselves as individuals in relation to each other and to the social group which the family becomes? What does parenthood mean to these people—what significance does the biological fact of fathering and mothering have, and what meanings do children come to have to their fathers and mothers?

It is to such self-definitions and concepts of participation (or lack of participation) in the family's life that we can trace many of the patterns of family planning and contraceptive practice described in the previous chapters. The relevance of these considerations appears in two ways. In terms of family planning goals, the number of children one has and the planning involved in having them achieve meaning from the ways married adults conceive of themselves as members of a family of procreation, and the ways they regard their spouses as members. With respect to contraceptive practices, the way in which contraception is executed from day to day will depend to a considerable extent on how husband and wife relate to each other, on how they see themselves and their partners in the marital relationship.

CONFLICT AND CO-OPERATION IN MARITAL ROLES

Planning at the Beginning of Marriage

The premarital relationship of the courtship period offers a first opportunity for the prospective husband and wife to choose and plan together. They choose each other, and together begin to build their lives according to implicit and explicit conceptions of what they are about as individuals and as a group. Courting signifies that the individual feels ready to decide as an adult, to make a lasting choice of a mate. Our culture favors this kind of self-determined choice, and our values about marriage include the idea that marriage should be contracted between a man and woman who freely choose each other, who have an independent desire to live together as man and wife. At the same time, the magnitude of the choice leads to considerable emotional upheaval.

For many women, choosing consciously is not so much the issue; they prefer to feel that they merely wait for their Prince Charming, and their choice is more the negative act of refusing those men who seem not to be what they seek. A woman may feel that she waits to be chosen—although the way she waits and the social situations and groups in which she waits do much to circumscribe the circle from which potential choosers come.

Given this over-all cultural pattern, however, there are many and varied ways in which choosing and planning do enter into courtship. Women need not be as passive as they seem, nor are men necessarily the most active pursuers of the married state. Our data suggest that in some courtships there is a sense of simply drifting together and very little awareness of personal choice in the decision to get married. Similarly, there is wide variation in the degree to which the courters plan their future together.

Many working class men and women, particularly those in the lower-lower class, give this impression of having just drifted together—they do not seem to have regarded themselves as active choosers of a mate but are inclined to think simply that it was about time to get married. Although it is unlikely that these people would have gotten married without some sense of personal meaningfulness to each other, it does seem that conscious choice and planning play a much smaller role than among middle class men and women. Some typical lower-lower class descriptions of courtship are these:

> I met him over on Lafflin street. There's a place I used to go to dance with a gang of us girls. These fellows always came around, too. I saw my husband lots of times before I went around with him. A bunch of us decided to go to the beach one night and he asked me. We fooled around and I liked the way he treated me. I don't know exactly how it happened; we got to going to the beach at night and fooling around some, and then we decided it would be best to get married right away [married 8 years, five children].
>
> We were neighbors together down in Kentucky. We grew up together. I knew her all my life. We went around together for about two years and just got married. I don't know why or how but we just did [married 11 years, four children].
>
> He stayed with his aunt in Kentucky and it was close to where I lived. I'd known him off and on for a year or two. I don't know how it come about, we just got married. I stayed home, then, and my husband just worked at a saw mill. After a couple of years we moved up here [married 9 years, four children].
>
> I was working in a theater as an usher. She came to the movie and we got acquainted. We went together for about a year and a half. Finally I couldn't take it, so I asked her to get married and I asked her parents. [Couldn't take it?] I wanted what any boy wanted when he was seventeen; she said no, I said yes, she won [married 12 years, four children].

Working class men and women do not often show a great deal of enterprise in seeking or choosing marriage partners. Rarely do they express strong feelings about the decision to marry. Resignation, a feeling that fate is dictating what is happening, and a lack of much elaboration in conscious planning and consideration are frequently reflected in the use of such phrases as "it was just time," "somehow it was settled," or "we just did it."

Most working class men and women seem to marry in profound ignorance of family planning issues; many have bits and pieces of information, but most seem to feel ill-prepared for events and decisions about sex and its consequences. To a considerable extent, adequacy of knowledge in this area seems a function of social status and social aspirations. The higher the status or the aspirations, the more likely it is that men or women will have something approaching adequate knowledge about sexual relations and conception. As might be expected, men generally tend to know more of the essential facts than women.

The typical lower class pattern among men includes at most the knowledge that men and women have sexual intercourse, that men enjoy it and women probably don't, that pregnancy results from having intercourse, and that contraception can be effected with a condom. The condom is useful especially before marriage to keep out of trouble if one is lucky enough to find a girl willing to have intercourse. Very little consideration seems to be given to family planning, and many lower class men seem to have thought of the condom before marriage mainly as an appliance to be used in premarital intercourse as a protection against disease and the proverbial shotgun.

Only infrequently do lower class couples discuss family planning or contraception before marriage. Sex is not discussed either; there may be some conflict over the man's desire for premarital intercourse, but it is an activity so surrounded with ambivalence and guilt that seldom does this problem lead to an explicit concern with sexuality or with family planning.

Common responses given by men to a question about premarital family planning and contraceptive information are these:

> Oh, I knew the usual things, the kinds of things that men would know of like prophylactics. I hadn't ever used any; it was just common knowledge, I guess. Just the things that boys pick up as part of growing up, and in service.
>
> I didn't know anything about it and I didn't give it any thought. When we had two kids about a year apart and neither of us knew anything, I went in the army and I read quite a bit about it and discussed it with a good many fellows and learned a lot.
>
> I didn't know nothing; I was twenty-one and my wife eighteen when we married. The first child was an accident, you might say, because I didn't know nothing about it. After the second we started talking. I went to the hospital and talked to the social worker.
>
> Well, I knew about rubbers and the Catholic way. The Catholic way I learned in church, the catechism and like that. I guess I learned about rubbers from the guys on the corner talking, you know, rubbers were the best thing if you dated a girl. As I got older I learned for myself.
>
> I knew very little before we got married, but right before we got a medical book and I read it through quite a bit and learned quite a bit about it.

Working class women, particularly those in the lower-lower class, generally have even less information about sex and contraception than do the men, and the women seem to give relatively little thought to spacing and limiting their families until some time after marriage. Very often they say that they have learned what they do know (usually about condoms) from their husbands since their marriage. It is not unusual for women in this group to say that they have never discussed the subject with anyone. On the other hand, quite a few lower class women have gotten information from female relatives *after* marriage; apparently discussions of sex and contraception are thought appropriate only among non-virgins. This consideration also seems to apply to those cases where relatives first discuss these matters with a prospective bride just before her wedding day. In any case, such discussions seem oriented to an "emergency," in the sense that the woman is shortly going to be forced to deal with an issue she would really prefer to ignore. These various patterns of learning or not learning are illustrated in our interviews by comments like the following:

> Girls talk about things like that—I knew about being careful before I was married. That's part of the reason I watch my girls so closely—more girls get themselves into trouble and expect the parents to get them out. I learned mostly after getting married, from my sisters-in-law, about douching and that. The rest I learned from the doctors and nurses at the clinic.
> I didn't know anything before I was married. Then my sister told me about douching, and I don't remember who told me about rubbers but it's something I never talked much about.
> I knew nothing when I got married. I didn't even know how a baby was born and how you got pregnant. My mother told me the night before I got married.
> I didn't know nothing about birth control before I got married. I learned from my husband. Just about the rubbers. He don't say nothing about any other stuff to me but that. He just uses rubbers. I haven't learned anything since. All my mother taught me ever was to not let boys get anywhere with me. She didn't explain nothing. She told me not to let boys be loving over me. She told me when I was about twelve; I didn't know what she meant. I guess she meant if they loved all over you what it would cause. I didn't know then but now I do. I didn't know about it until I was married.
> I knew nothing about babies or how to have or not have them before I was married. I didn't really know it. I heard it but I didn't read no books. I learned by experience of being married. I always thought you had to see a doctor before you got pregnant. My husband never discussed it with me before we were married. I didn't know the act led to pregnancy.

Women who have a more thorough knowledge tend to be in the upper-lower class rather than in the lower-lower group, and they also more often have been reared in an urban environment. In general, those couples who manage to be effective at contraception before they have too many children know more about contraception and the facts of reproduction before they are married. Their behavior in marriage is based on information acquired before marriage and supplemented later. This is not to say that all the couples who have been effective were informed about contraception before marriage; a minority of the early-planner group learn later, as do many of those who become effective at contraception in desperation after having four or five children.

It is difficult to believe that a sizable minority of these women did not know at marriage that sexual intercourse leads to pregnancy. Perhaps it is rather that the whole question of sexuality was so anxiety-laden for them that they effectively pushed the issue aside in their minds and managed to ignore it completely, so that the relevance of sexual intercourse to their lives after marriage came as a real shock to them. Actually, many lower class men seem almost as effectively to isolate sexuality in the sense of a pleasurable "lay" from their thinking about a family and children. They do not so often repress the facts as do lower class women, but they seem unable to use their knowledge constructively in considering the impending marriage. In any case, our data suggest that consciously usable knowledge is woefully lacking for most working class couples and that a lack of consideration of the sex-planning-contraception constellation of issues results in tension and misunderstanding in the early period of marriage.

Conceptions of the Good Husband and the Good Wife

Each partner in a marriage has certain expectations of himself and of his spouse; he feels that both of them must do certain things and behave in certain ways if they are to be good partners. The activities of a husband and wife can be roughly categorized into a number of roles he must play; if these are played well, he can consider himself to have done well. The activities which constitute each role must somehow mesh with those of the spouse in a co-operative and complementary fashion. In order to gain an overview of the way our respondents felt about these various roles, we asked the men and women we interviewed to rank in importance the roles a husband or wife is expected to fulfill. The roles included the parental function (a good father or mother to the children), work activities (a good provider or housekeeper), being a good lover (the same for both sexes), and being a good friend (the same for both sexes). We will discuss the results briefly before going on to a more dynamic analysis of the ways in which working class people think of themselves as husbands and wives.

The concept of "the good husband" seems to be somewhat different for men and women. Men tend to give first importance to being a good father, but few women do. Instead, women are more likely to want their husbands first of all to be either good providers or good lovers. Men generally rate being a good provider second in importance, so that for them the couplet father-provider includes the really important elements of being a good father. For a good number of women, particularly those in the lower-lower class, their husbands' orientation is quite contrary to their own wishes. Three-fifths of the lower-lower class women in our sample ranked being a good lover first or second in importance for a good husband, yet less than 5 per cent of the lower-lower class husbands ranked this role as high, and three-fifths of them put it in the "least important" category.

The concept of "the good wife" is similarly open to disagreement. Men sharply restrict the definition of a good wife to the mother-housekeeper components. It would seem that for both the good husband and the good wife, men tend to adhere quite closely to fairly formal, non-affectional definitions of what is important. Women do not so often like to think of themselves as mainly mothers and housekeepers. Wives seem to want to avoid so heavily limiting the marital relationship to the parental; they attribute less importance to both fatherliness and motherliness than do men. Perhaps they are so much with their children that they take their own motherly activities more for granted that the husbands do, and perhaps also they prefer their husbands to tend to other matters and leave the children to mother. Women rate being a good housewife even lower; they prefer to concentrate on the interpersonal qualities of loving, or being a good friend or mother.

Thus there emerges a pattern in which the expectations each spouse has of the other and of himself differ significantly: what wives think important in their husbands, the husbands tend to underemphasize, and what husbands think important in the way their wives act as wives, the wives themselves tend to underemphasize. We have noted that on the whole, lower class men seem to have a much more concrete, unemotional, sharply defined conception of the proper functioning of husband and wife in the family than have the wives. Husbands tend to define the family as a unit in which both function to operate a little business (the husband brings in money and the wife manages the home) and to rear children. While—as we shall see in more detail in the following sections—the wives share these values, they are more likely to insist that other things are important for a good marriage.

Lower class wives seem to have strong needs for affection which their husbands do not recognize. Husbands emphasize functions which, while complementary, are parallel—the husband goes to work, the wife works at home; the husband relates to the children as a father, the wife as a mother. Women highlight the importance of such interactive functions as love-making and friendship. In the actual marriage relationship, it is probably easier for the wife to go along with her husband than it is for her to persuade him to interact more affectionately—both because it is difficult for one person to force affection from another and because the wife already is persuaded that the parental and work roles are important, while the husband may be quite insensitive to the wife's affectional needs.

One result is that in most working class families sharing experience tends to be limited. Each partner becomes a specialist in certain tasks and sees the other in specialized roles. This emphasis on formal, impersonal roles results in a sense of distance, an attitude of "O.K., you stick to your job and I'll stick to mine." Still, the affectional needs of the wife are not met and less conscious needs of the husband for intimate contact are also unmet. (It is quite possible that the husband's strong emphasis on the mother role harbors some wish that his wife might mother him, too.) In such a situation there is much room for conflict; each partner may operate at cross-purposes to the other, and misunderstandings may arise in whatever efforts are made to establish common family goals. As Hess and Handel (1959) have commented:

> Living together, the individuals in a family each develop an image of what the other members are like. Referring to one person's emotionalized conception of another, an image is shaped both by the holder and the object. . . . While it represents the holder's needs and wishes, it also represents the object as a source of fulfillment. Each family member has some kind of image of every other member and of himself in relation to them.

Further, each family must establish for themselves a satisfactory congruence of images through interaction and mutual affirmation of what each is to himself and to the others. When the images of family members are congruent, that is, when the expectations and meanings which members have of each other fit together in a functional way, the family goes along smoothly. When this is not so, when, for example, there is a lack of congruence between the image a wife holds of herself and that which her husband holds of her, then difficulty and conflict are likely to ensue. When, as seems often to be the case in these lower class marriages, the wife wishes to be regarded as a person who needs and gives love and affection and the husband feels that she is simply a good mother and housekeeper, both partners are likely to feel disappointed, cheated, and misunderstood. When one family member emphasizes one or two roles to the exclusion of others, his spouse is likely to feel limited, fenced in, imprisoned by the image the other holds.

The conceptions described above are common in the lower class generally and probably have much to do with the family planning troubles characteristic of the group. The lack of closeness between husband and wife sometimes serves to delay family planning until the stage of desperation and to interfere with smoothness in executing plans to limit the family's size once some decision is made.

When we examine the role rankings made by effective and ineffective users of contraceptives of the same sex, we find some important differences. Women who are effective in limiting family size emphasize the lover role more often than ineffective women. This is not limited to one or the other partner as lover. In the whole group, 70 per cent of the effective women rank "lover" as most or next most important for either the good husband or the good wife, while only 21 per cent of the ineffective contraceptive users do so. Apparently if the wife is able to face loving (in either its direct sexual or more attenuated forms) as an important issue in marriage for at least one of the partners, it is more likely that she will be able to be effective at contraception. In most cases this probably comes about through her greater ability to accept sexuality as a legitimate part of marriage and therefore to deal directly with contraception in connection with sexual relations.

Among men, the pattern is more complex. Over three-quarters of the men in our sample put the couplets of father-provider and mother-housewife first in their judgments, and there are no differences in this respect between effective and ineffective men. We do find, however, that whether the man regards the husband's lover role as more or less important than his friend role is related to effectiveness in family limitation. Among the effective ones, 65 per cent rank being a good lover as *less* important than being a good friend, while among the ineffective ones, 79 per cent rank "lover" as being *more* important. This makes sense when we consider that one of the important elements in effective contraceptive practice is that the husband be considerate of his wife's desire not to have more children than she feels she can bear or care for. Another important element is that he must be able to handle his sexual desires in ways which permit contraception. A "good friend" will show this kind of consideration. It seems likely that the ineffective husbands who rank "lover" higher than "friend" take "being a good lover" in a narcissistic sense to mean self-enjoyment in making love, and pride themselves on their sexuality more than on their solicitude toward their wives.

Conceptions of Self and Other in Marriage

It will prove fruitful to examine in more depth the underlying conceptions which husbands and wives have of themselves in their relations to their spouses and the images each has of the other. The following data come primarily from projective materials and from those parts of our interviews in which the respondent was asked to describe himself as a person and to describe his spouse. We will note certain aspects of the images characteristic of the working class in general and then examine some of the differences between effective and ineffective contraceptive users.

Working class wives' conceptions of the husband-wife relationship have been extensively described in *Workingman's Wife* (Rainwater, Coleman, and Handel, 1959); we will summarize these findings here as they apply to our particular interest. These women find it difficult to think of themselves in any other status than a familial one. One of the reasons they marry at an early age is that when they outgrow the status of daughter they feel somewhat lost and look forward to the clear-cut status of wife and mother as a way of securely establishing themselves as *someone* again. Their husbands become central to their lives as the main source of security, both emotional and social. Being married, having a husband, reassures the woman that she has a respectable place in society; being a good wife to her husband fosters a sense of being a worthwhile person with some meaningful purpose, and of being a real woman.

Yet working class wives typically feel isolated from their husbands in many ways; often they are not sure exactly what the trouble is, but they feel unsure and vaguely uncomfortable about their ties to their husbands. Most centrally, they are doubtful about their hold on their husbands and very anxious about asserting themselves against the husband lest he go away; they fear that he will seek gratification elsewhere, either temporarily or permanently. "Holding one's man" becomes a major goal for many working class wives, and they generally think holding him requires that they give in to his wishes as much as possible.

These views these women hold are grounded in their conceptions of the nature of men; their husbands are representatives of the general category of men, perhaps better than most but nevertheless to be dealt with in terms of "the way men are." For most of these women, men are seen as dominant and controlling. They are, like the rest of the external world, unpredictable, difficult to understand, and more powerful than the women. They are not easily managed; it is difficult for working class wives to feel that they effectively control the actions of men. Further, men withhold affection; they are inconsiderate and insensitive. One cannot expect much from men unless one is very lucky. These women often settle for permanence in a not-too-happy relationship because they feel nothing better is to be had from a man; indeed, one is lucky if he will just stay around.

It follows that it is hard to change a man's ways. He is an independent and egocentric person who, if pressed too hard, will simply go away. Often, these wives resign themselves to all-or-none ways of dealing with their men. Until things become impossibly bad they simply resign themselves; if the situation is unbearable, the wife is justified in leaving her husband. The middle ground of negotiation, give-and-take, and mutual understanding requires both too much faith in the basic goodness of men and too much assertiveness on the woman's part to be readily considered.

In all of this, these women feel quite inferior to men, and they have considerable admiration of maleness as enabling its possessor to go his own way and do as he pleases. It is comforting to have such a person around, but it is also frustrating, since these wives have so few techniques for managing the relationship in ways that will prove emotionally gratifying. Given these views, it is not difficult to understand why so many working class wives acquiesce to isolation from their husbands and to separate, parallel functioning in the family rather than real sharing. Although they feel unhappy about their isolation, they feel that the man prefers it, and perhaps it is better anyway since they are not required to expose themselves to the anxiety and rejection likely to follow more active approaches to their husbands.

The differences between effective and ineffective practitioners are more of degree than kind. Both groups show the same intense concern in their relationships to their husbands, and both show insecurity about their holds on their husbands. There are differences, however, in the severity of isolation and insecurity the two groups of women feel, and also in the assertiveness they are able to bring to bear in coping with their problems.

Ineffective women have the greatest sense of estrangement and isolation in relating to their husbands, and they feel most hopeless about effectively approaching them. Some examples of how these wives describe their husbands will illustrate their range of images:

> My husband stinks. He gives us nothing. He hardly ever works. He don't pay no attention to the kids and all he does is smoke and drink beer. I guess we get along as well as most people do [!]. If we had some money we could be happier. With five kids to feed it's tough, but my oldest boy is a good boy. He delivers papers and gives me his money. [Married sixteen years.]
>
> I don't know how to describe him. I just can't. He's just a man. He's really interested in cars and he likes to fish. Now he's a mechanic; he loves his work. He's always fixing the neighbors' cars for nothing. I get mad about it but he don't listen to me. [Good points?] Well [thinks for a long time], when he gets off he takes me and the kids for a ride sometime; that's better than most, I guess. He don't want to take us but he'd rather do that than argue. [Bad points?] His friends hang around here all the time, or he just goes off with them. He gets along good with the kids but he isn't around much. I get along pretty good with him, I guess. It used to be better but with three kids and all, we keep getting farther and farther apart. [Married four years, three children.]
>
> He's the quiet type but he drinks too much and has too much desire for sexual relations, I think. He likes baseball and TV. He's a good provider, works hard and usually brings his money home. He's good to me and the children. I guess the main bad point is his drinking. He doesn't drink too much during the week but an awful lot on the weekends when he's home. I don't feel we can afford it, and he gets rather rough and loud when he's drinking. I get along with him as well as most husbands and wives do, I guess. I fuss at him for drinking and he fusses at me for fussing at him. [Married fifteen years, five children and very unhappy at being pregnant again.]

Each of these women expresses in terms of her own reality the point of view previously outlined. The first woman finds her husband impossible, but she does not really think other couples are much better off. The second is learning wistfully to put up with the isolation her husband's other interests force on her. The third contends with her husband's drinking but does not think she can do anything about it.

In general, the sense of separation and poor communication with their husbands that exists among the ineffective wives is striking. They feel they do not really understand their men; they find them impulsive and given to inexplicable anger or other forms of striking out. They worry that perhaps their husbands do not find them appealing; they fear that basically they are unappealing to men in general. They do not like to give in to their men against their own better judgment or preferences, but they have very little confidence that the men will stay with them if they are demanding. Since they lack techniques for controlling the relationship, they have a general sense of failure and tend to fall to the level of nagging, subtle punishment (particularly in the sexual area), pointless minor conflicts, and minding their own business. Typically, as we shall see, they turn their attention and loving impulses toward their children.

Effective women, while not dramatically different since they also are preoccupied with holding their men and uncertain about doing so, feel that they have a more active role in their common life with their husbands. They see themselves as of greater concern to their husbands than simply as conveniences—mere caretakers of the household and convenient sexual objects when desired. These women find it easier to think of themselves as taking the center of the stage in the family, maintaining responsible standards in family life, and setting goals which their husbands can be expected to live up to. Typically, they are able to be more maternal in their attitudes toward men, and they feel themselves less subordinated to men's gross preferences. In this sense they come closer to middle-class patterns by insisting on the maintenance of such values as virtue, niceness, cleanliness, neatness, financial stability, etc. In short, these women give the impression of being more engaged in their relations with their husbands, and they think of men as more engaged also. They may have difficulties and frictions, but they have not got the deep hopelessness about a constructive outcome of their lives together that characterizes the ineffective group.

Typically, effective women give a more balanced pro-and-con picture of their husbands, and they are distinctly more complimentary about some aspects of male personality even when they criticize others. Even though they feel that husbands must be handled with care, they seem to feel that they themselves count for more in the marital relationship. Typical descriptions of their husbands by lower-lower class effective women are these:

> I don't know what to say; I think you can describe him as just good. He's good, kind, and considerate. We don't always have enough money to go around, but we have enough love to go around. We don't have much furniture; we have things that his mother and my mother had for years, but we've got enough love in our home to fill the gap between new furniture and old furniture. [His interests?] He likes to work on old cars; I think he likes that better than anything else. [Bad points?] He's so particular about his food; he's not somebody that anybody can cook for and you almost have to be able to iron perfect which I'm not. [Good points?] He doesn't drink. We have our arguments as all married people do, but we have our agreements as well as disagreements. [Married eight years, three children.]
>
> He's a friendly type person and real easy to live with. He likes hunting and fishing and he has beehives that he likes to fool with. He really doesn't drink at all so that's a good point. He gets along well with the children, and I know you won't believe this but we've never had a bad argument. [Married 17 years, three children.]
>
> He has a wonderful personality; he's handsome and a wonderful father to the kids. He plays with them and always has time to spend with them. He likes golf and bowling; he plays with the fellows from work. [Bad points?] He likes to gamble and he curses. We don't have much money and he still gambles. I've given up fussing about it so we get along real good now. I'm sure he loves me and feels I'm the stuff! I'm very happy and wouldn't trade married life for anything. [Married five years, three children.]

Drinking seems to be an issue about which many working class wives are concerned. For many of these women, alcohol comes to symbolize the main threat to the stability of their marriages; husbands who drink are even more likely than men in general to prove destructive, unreliable and unfaithful. Therefore, it is a point of pride to many working class women that their husbands drink moderately or not at all. On the other hand, women whose husbands enjoy drinking are anxious and worried, often nagging their husbands regularly about it. It is interesting, therefore, that ineffective women complain about their husbands' drinking much more often than effective women. Among ineffective women, fully 60 per cent complain that their husbands drink, while only 12 per cent of the effective women criticize their husbands on this score.

Like their wives, working class husbands find the world around them confusing and chaotic; they do not feel that they understand it, and they feel that what goes on is essentially unpredictable, up to fate. Women are, of course, part of that world and characterized by the same unpredictableness and confusing qualities as the rest of it. Also like the women, these men find it difficult to think of themselves as effective, mastering agents in their world; they simply hope things go well and do their best with the resources they have.

Working class men, even more than men in general, tend to think of women as temperamental, emotional, demanding, and irrational; they are sometimes in deadly earnest when they, with the hero of *My Fair Lady*, ask with exasperation, "Why can't a woman be more like a man?" They think that women do silly things: they cry for no reason, they argue in petty ways about the things a man wants to do, and they are always acting hurt for no apparent reason.

Even more threatening, women are clinging and very emotional about wanting their men to be affectionate—they are sticky and won't leave a man alone unless he insists. Many of these men find their wives' demands for affection irritating and threatening. They do not know quite how to respond, and they seem anxious to avoid getting in too deeply by going along with their wives—it is as if they feared that they might not be able to provide all that women want were they to try.

Yet because they want things from their wives, they are reluctant to pull away completely. It is important to them, too, to be married, since that is the proper state for a grown man. Further, being married is convenient; it provides gratifications in a secure and stable way and wards off one's anxieties about the unpredictable, likely-to-be-ungiving world. The man who is not married has to be even more energetic in seeking the basic goods he wants—he must have someone to feed him, to take care of his clothes, to provide him with a comfortable atmosphere in which to watch TV, to allow him sexual gratification.

These husbands often resort to various kinds of blustering, aggressive tactics with their wives in order to gain the gratifications they want and at the same time have the woman keep her proper distance. Each likes to think of himself as master of the house, and he plays on his wife's capacity to be intimidated by aggressive actions and threats to withdraw. But, of course, these men want to do well by their wives and their families. As we have seen, they like to think of themselves as good providers and good fathers. If they can think of themselves in this way, they feel entitled to some of the self-indulgent gratifications about which the wives complain—drinking a little, cultivating a masculine hobby, getting away with the boys on hunting and fishing trips. They tend to shy away from the demands of close integration into the family life and prefer to stay a little on the side. In this sense, many of the feelings their wives have about them as isolated by self-indulgent concerns are quite realistic.

Yet the men often feel guilty and vaguely inadequate about their behavior as husbands. Much of their aggressive blustering serves to defend them against feelings of not having done well by the family, as does much of their withdrawal into strictly masculine concerns. This guilt may account for their touchiness in many areas of husbandly responsibility, for their wariness, and for their tendency to gloss matters over both in discussions within the family and in their stance toward the outside world (this includes our interviewers; we found men much more evasive respondents than women).

One central motive is apparent in the underlying wishes these men have about their wives—they would very much like to be mothered. Often in describing their wives they speak of them as not only good mothers to the children but also to themselves:

> My wife has a lot of good qualities, being nice to me, keeps my clothing clean, cooks for all of us, and gets along good with all of our children.
> She is very careful about money and does not waste it. She's a good housekeeper, a good cook, and good to me and the kids.
> She is a good woman; she makes friends easy, is good to me and the kids, and does not kick about what I do. She takes good care of the children and cooks and does a little housework for other people sometimes—she is good to all of us.
> She keeps the children and the house clean and does not waste money on things we do not need. About her only bad point is she does not like food and I do, and she does not cook enough for me.

In the role of housewife obviously inhere many motherly functions, and it is apparent that these are quite meaningful to working class men. They want to be taken care of, and they want not to have to worry about what goes on at home; this leaves them free to direct their energies along more "masculine" lines.

These men make a sharp distinction between good and bad women. Good women are basically mothers; they run households, take care of children and of husbands. While they are receptive to their husbands sexually, they do not independently seek sexual gratification. Good women stay at home and are not too interested in what goes on in the outside world. Bad women, of course, are mainly interested in sex, and are to be found mostly in bars and hotel rooms. They drink a lot and are very likely to get a man in trouble at the same time that they offer him pleasure. A man is better off if he can have sexual gratification at home and avoid such women. Women should be one or the other, but sometimes, according to working class men, a good woman goes bad. It is reasonable for a husband to keep close watch over his wife so that this does not happen to her.

It is apparent that much of the tension in working class marriages comes from the conflicting demands the spouses make on each other. The husband is frightened by and does not understand some of his wife's desires for affection. To the extent that these are sexually phrased, he is uneasy lest this be an indication that she may become a bad woman. For his part, he wants mothering without being made to feel subordinate to his wife. He wants nurturance and care; he also wants to be free to go his own way when he wishes. The wife perceives his desires for mothering as demanding (although she also knows that this is her best way of holding him) and feels cheated since she does not receive the full measure of protection and affection she desires in return.

In our sample, ineffective men show strong tendencies toward casualness and looseness in their ties to other people, and particularly to women. They are more apt to derogate women in general, and they are not sure that good women are really good. They have a sneaking suspicion that all women are likely to go bad if one doesn't watch out. They are often quite hostile to their wives, particularly toward their non-motherly aspects. They tend to have little empathy with people and to see others as governed largely by self-seeking and gross aims.

These men strongly avoid guilt and show little tolerance for guilty feelings. Their tendency is to act impulsively and then move away rapidly from any situation in which the consequences of impulsive action might make them feel guilty. Their view that things just happen anyway, that people are inexplicable most of the time, further protects them from the direct experience of guilt because of transgressions. Their motivations are simply and primitively conceived. People do things because of money, because of sex, or because they've been drinking. Sex is regarded as a getting-on-and-getting-off experience with little elaboration. It is a good idea to get away from the woman as quickly as possible—to run or to retreat into oneself—in order to avoid consequences and possible demands.

Effective men, while not greatly different, show more sensitivity to women and their needs and are more likely to see marriage as creating an integrated unit in which they have a central rather than a peripheral role. They are more aware of their own guilt feelings and more cognizant of the possibilities of retribution for misbehavior. They are not quite so unrealistic in believing that they can run away. While they, too, often find "immorality" tempting, they back away for fear of repercussions instead of acting impulsively. They show less fascination with drinking as a way of forgetting their inhibitions and are more likely to think that drinking interferes with interpersonal gratification.

They see relationships with women as more interdependent and avoid them less. They are more tolerant of the idea that a man must care for a woman and look after her, and more receptive to her demands for care. In general, they are not as derogating in their attitudes toward women. While they also maintain a sharp dichotomy between good and bad women, they do not believe good women backslide so easily. Responsiveness to a wife's legitimate demands and willingness to maintain the marriage tie are, to them, one's duty to the good woman.

THE MEANING OF PARENTHOOD

Two aspects of being a parent are important in connection with family planning: the meaning of the biological fact of becoming a parent, and the meaning and function of children in the lives of their parents. The first has to do with very deeply felt conceptions of oneself as a man or a woman, the second with the ramified ways in which the psychosocial identity of father or mother is defined in action.

The Ability to Have Children

To impregnate and to become pregnant signify to the individual a kind of categorical maturity as adult human beings; the natural consequence of sexual intercourse fixes more permanently and obviously than can the private experience of love-making the status of adulthood, of being grown up. For the working class, which lives much closer to biological experience than does the middle class, the experience of having children assumes heightened importance, and around this fact much of their lives revolve.

For the prospective mother the impact is naturally greatest. As Simone de Beauvoir (1949) notes, "It is in maternity that woman fulfills her physiological destiny; it is her natural 'calling,' since her whole organic structure is adapted for the perpetuation of the species." Among working class women, as noted in detail elsewhere (Rainwater, Coleman, and Handel, 1959), having children looms very large in their efforts to assure themselves of being respectable and worthwhile; if becoming a wife makes a woman feel that she has established herself as a good woman, becoming a mother clinches the argument and also marks the final establishment of her separation from her own mother (Deutsch, 1933). Becoming pregnant represents a fulfillment of herself against which arguments cannot be brought; she categorically *is* a mother and therefore *is not* other things she fears she might have been—a person of no consequence, a bad person, or a person with no purpose. Motherhood is much more completely her reason for being than it is for the middle class woman, who is taught the value of outside interests for establishing her validity as a person.

The experience of pregnancy and childbirth, then, has heightened significance for working class women—it is absorbing and fascinating in a complete way, and it comes to be the most eventful experience in their lives. Again and again, our respondents speak of it in this way:

> I got along fine during pregnancy. It gave me a lot of satisfaction in being able to have the things I wanted—I mean children.
>
> I think it is one of the things you look forward to in your life. I think it is a great experience. It's worth anything when you see the baby.
>
> I take spinals and watch them being born. It's just wonderful. It's so wonderful, especially after you feel life. I guess I'm just a mother and a homebody; I love children.

Since these women look to pregnancy as a kind of natural, completely absorbing experience that establishes for all the world to see their legitimacy as mature females, it is understandable that many working class women's first anxiety does not concern having too many children but having none at all. Most of our respondents do not begin to think of family planning and limitation until they are convinced of their fecundity. Their uncertainty about themselves and their lack of trust in the world means that they are often not sure enough of their capacity to have children to be able to plan when to have them and how many to have. First they must prove their capability to themselves and their husbands.

The central significance of pregnancy in their lives does not, of course, mean that it is always a pleasurable experience. Many of the women we interviewed seemed to have a great deal of difficulty with pregnancy, difficulty which may have as much to do with uncertainties and conflicts about themselves and about an ungiving world as with more strictly physiological factors. Particularly among women who have had more children than they want we find complaints about the difficulties and painfulness of pregnancy, and also a good deal of anger at husbands inconsiderate enough to force their wives to become pregnant. When the wife begins to feel that "having babies seems to be the only thing that ever happens in my life and I feel so miserable when I'm that way," she may begin contraception in desperation, but often she has difficulty in persuading her husband that things have to change.

For the prospective father, pregnancy has many of the same meanings as for the wife, but more vaguely, since *he* does not change. The full meaning of having impregnated a woman probably develops only when the husband has some capacity for identifying with his wife. We have noted that many lower class men have difficulty in empathizing with women, so that pregnancy and childbearing often remain for them mysterious, frightening, and vaguely unsettling. The man may react to his anxiety with increased solicitude: "Having children has never been too bad for my wife. She isn't sick very much, and when she is I take better care of her than ever." He may also react by withdrawing farther from the family and pursuing his own interests. In general, the former seems the more typical reaction; indeed, many women indicated that the only time they really felt their husbands close to them and deeply interested in them was when they were pregnant. When this is the case, it is easy to see that motivation to limit pregnancies is reduced. In return, some working class women seem to become more interested in sexual relations during pregnancy; they often rationalize this by saying that they do not have to worry about becoming pregnant since they already are.

Having his wife become pregnant is proof to the man that he is *really* "potent"—that he has the capacity not only to have orgasms but also to impregnate—just as the wife feels more confidently grown up when she becomes pregnant (Stycos, 1955). For the working class man, however, this proof of masculinity is much less absorbing than the wife's proof of femininity, and he is also more uncertain of it. Lower class men's interest in having many children may have much to do with their need for repeated proof of potency. Since they tend to feel ineffective and weak in relation to their world, fathering a string of children comes to represent a kind of defiant demonstration that they are real men.

Given their ideas about good and bad women, having a pregnant wife serves an important function in reassuring these men that their wives are good women, since "mother" and "good woman" are synonymous to them. If the wife is kept a full-time mother, with a series of pregnancies and many children, the husband feels reassured that she cannot change into a bad woman when he is not looking. Such feelings probably account for some of his apparent insensitivity to his wife's desire for no more children.

Also, since potency is an aggressive experience for many lower class men, there is a definitely hostile component to impregnation, symbolized in the phrase "knocked up" which some of our respondents used to describe their wives' pregnancies. The hostility which (as we will see in the next chapter) many of these men express in their sexual behavior comes to complete fulfillment in the suffering which the wife may have in pregnancy and childbirth, and even later in caring for more children than she would like. Many of the ineffective wives perceive their husbands' attitudes as this kind of hostile indifference to the painful consequences of having more children and to the problems of child-rearing:

> Sure, my husband likes it when he doesn't have to put on a rubber, and he likes me to be pregnant for some reason, but he knows how much work there is to a new baby and how much everything costs, and that ought to stop him but it doesn't. [Married eight years, five children.]
>
> He don't care how many children we have. He wouldn't care if there was one every time we went to bed; he don't do nothing to keep them from coming. The satisfaction is all on his part. I've never felt any pleasure from being with a man,

but he sure must get something, as often as he wants me! I've almost died every time I've been pregnant; every one has been a breech birth. What I go through never fazed him; the children themselves are the only satisfaction I ever got out of the deal. [Married 19 years, four children.]

For both husbands and wives, then, the connection between being a mature and potent member of one's sex and having children serves to delay a concern with family planning. The delay is longer for men than for women, since women have brought home to them more fully the deep gratifications of child-bearing and rearing, and also the pains and troubles. Both for reasons of anxiety about one's masculinity and because of hostile, aggressive feelings toward women, many working class men chafe at effective measures for preventing pregnancies.

The Value and Function of Children

Once children have arrived, they take on different meanings; they come to be individuals to whom one must relate and whose independent existence must be taken into account in the way the husband and wife live. The relatively simple meanings which *having* children represent become much more complex as the children become psychosocial realities as well as biological events. Several differences in the meanings children have and in attitudes toward them occur between effective and ineffective users of contraception.

To the working class mother, caring for children represents the central activity of her life. She defines herself mainly as a mother and seeks to find gratification in life principally through this function. The children are considered mainly her property and responsibility, and it is through them that she expects to fulfill herself and her potentialities; if her children love her now and in the future, she feels she has gained the only really important gratification which her world allows her.

There are a number of qualitative differences in the way effective and ineffective lower class women regard both their roles as mothers and their children. Because the ineffective women feel more isolated from their husbands, they tend to be more extreme than effective mothers in setting up a family which consists of mother and children with the husband as a necessary but distant appendage. Children come to represent an avenue of compensation for their husbands' lack of affection. The ineffective women tend to develop intense relationships with their children in order to gain interpersonal gratification and a sense of being worthwhile, since their husbands tend to treat them indifferently. When, for example, a woman experiences the kind of rejection illustrated in the following quotation, she is inclined to turn in desperation to her children for some sense of being valued and loved:

> I don't like my husband to run off all the time, and I nag about it. He never lets me go out alone, so why should I let him. I've been downtown two times since we've been married [four years], and I took the kids with me then. One night last year my husband said he'd take me out. The lady next door said she'd watch the kids. We got down to the corner and my husband said he was too tired. He took me right back home. I never was so mad in all my life! One time we could have gone out alone and he was too tired! I guess he's happy with the way I treat the children, but once I was real sick, and when he came home the kids were dirty and he really got mad.

Even when the sense of distance in the marital relation is not so great, these women often find it easier to relate to their children in affectionate ways than to their husbands. The children (at least when young) seem easier to manage and arouse fewer conflicts than does the difficult task of relating to grown men whom they do not understand too well and of whom they are often a little afraid.

Children are seen mainly as pleasurable objects and are valued for the day-to-day sense of well-being they provide. In the working class generally, and particularly among the ineffective group, we find relatively little orientation to the long-range goals in child-rearing which are so important in the middle class mother's attitudes toward her children. These women tend instead to take the attitude that if the home is "happy" from day to day, they are doing their jobs well and all is for the best.

When there are more children than the woman would have preferred—when she finds herself saddled with the care of five or six children, for example—even the compensatory gratifications of motherhood are likely to sour. The labor and emotional drain of children then come to outweigh the gratifications they offer. The desperate planners discussed earlier often fit this pattern. A second and a third child may have given the mother a greater sense of emotional absorption and a distraction from frustrations in her relations with her husband, but more children become a burden; the woman feels caught between her husband's demands for a troublefree home and the children's for attention, mothering, and things that cost money. At times like these the mother begins to feel that having more children than one wants is unfair because "you feel kind of hard toward the babies."

Working class women who succeed in effectively planning their families before they reach the desperate stage tend to have a stronger perception of the child as an individual. As noted in Chapter iv, they are more likely to think of the importance of giving the child the average American advantages of housing, clothing, and education, and less likely to make a decision to have more or fewer children merely to maintain an adequate level of subsistence. While the child may still be important to them as an avenue of simpler emotional gratification, their ability to invest in the individual makes them less anxious to have "lots of kids" around and more sensitive to the real difficulties of rearing a large family. Where, for example, the mothers have social aspirations for their children, they are likely to be especially aware of the advantages of limiting their number and of spacing births in order to be able to do well for any new addition to the family.

To the working class father, children represent a much more peripheral aspect of his work. A great deal of these men's energy is taken up with work and work concerns. While they do not, like middle class men, throw themselves into "careers" (they tend, rather, to think of "jobs"), their underlying uncertainties about the stability of their world and their feelings of inadequacy in coping with it mean that they are preoccupied with work, and very often it serves as a distraction from home. Given the sense of effort they have about work, they are inclined to seek self-indulgent activities which take them away from the family, often physically removing them from home in leisure time, more often psychologically withdrawing them from interaction with their family into television or some interesting hobby.

At the same time, as we have seen earlier, these men need to think of themselves as good providers and good fathers. They like to feel that they oversee the operation of a well-run home, that their wives serve them well by being good mothers and housekeepers. Even so, the realities of interaction in the house suggest that they often prefer to let their wives run things as long as they are not bothered by what happens.

It is apparent in our data that the main difference between husbands who are effective contraceptive users and those who are not is that the former are more involved in the family's activities, that they participate more fully as fathers, and that they pride themselves more on active fatherhood as opposed to categorical fatherhood, i.e., simply *being* fathers. Thus, when asked to tell the interviewer what kind of person he is, the effective husband is much more likely to mention some characteristic in connection with his fatherly activities than is the ineffective husband. Clearly, while the status of being a "good father" is something that both groups value, the activities of fatherhood are more meaningful to the effective group.

The underlying attitude of the ineffective father seems to be, "I do the best I can, and I'm entitled to relax the way I like without interference from my family." These lower class men can be quite touchy about their wives' criticisms, but they tend to pursue their own interests and not to find family participation really gratifying. One gets the impression that their involvement in such hobbies as car tinkering and joy riding or in drinking are often ways of running both from their preoccupations with their effectiveness as job-holders and providers and from the sense of frustration and irritation they feel because of their wives' and childrens' demands. Because they tend to run from the family, they are not particularly sensitive to its needs or to their wives' problems in having more children than are wanted.

The effective fathers express a variety of concerns in connection with their fatherhood and phrase their pride at being good fathers in a variety of ways. Some emphasize the importance of earning enough money to give their wives and children all that they need. Others emphasize the time they spend with the children and the interest they take in their development. Some speak of their role as disciplinarian, and still others of the love and affection they receive from the children. In describing themselves as individuals, effective fathers mention their fatherly concerns in these ways:

> One thing about me, I see that my family gets what they need before anything else; I've made that a rule ever since I've been married. [Your good points?] I am good to the kids and try to make a good life for them.
>
> My kids love me and I love them. They're really nice kids, you know.
>
> [Good points?] I'm a good father, provider, and husband. A good father corrects his children; a woman can't do it and they might get in the wrong crowd and environment.
>
> I like to take the boys fishing quite a lot on weekends. I don't like to live in town; I'd rather be out in the country with

> the kids. I get along good with the boys and do a lot of things with them like fishing, playing baseball, and we go out in the country a lot and have a good time together. The little girl [1½ years] is not old enough to do much yet.
> I like to take the boys with me when I go fishing. I try to make money and keep my wife and family happy and do not run around by myself and get drunk or stay out late at night.

This last man makes quite clear the two alternatives traditional in the lower class—one runs around and gets drunk, or one pays attention to one's family. It is a matter of considerable pride to many effective fathers, as is apparent in the remarks quoted above, that they have chosen the moral alternative.

The ineffective fathers are much less likely to mention anything connected with fatherhood until prodded by a question which asks about the children. Their spontaneous characterizations generally end with some discussion of work and recreational interests:

> Well, I've been working ever since I was big enough to work—I ran a pool room for three years, worked on a farm for seven years, and I've been working in a factory for about four years. I like fishing, hunting, and all sports. I spend too much money on foolishness. I like nice cars. [Relation to wife?] Well, I think everything goes pretty well; of course, we all have our quarrels in different matters. [Children?] Well, they're just boys, I guess.

Though sporadically they may spend time with the children, their participation seems based mainly on personal whim and enjoyment rather than on a desire for close relationships within the family.

chapter vi

MUTUALITY AND REJECTION IN SEXUAL RELATIONS

T RADITIONALLY, sexual intercourse is an activity appropriate only to marital partners, as its various synonyms—e.g., "the conjugal act"—imply. The appropriateness is both exclusive and positive: unmarried persons should not have sexual relations, and married persons must if the marriage is to be considered consummated. Sexual intercourse, then, is "one of the things marriage is all about," a point of view expressed in many ways by our respondents.

Since sex is one of the cornerstones of marriage, we can expect to learn much about the quality of particular marital relationships by examining the ways husbands and wives regard their sexual relations. Because coitus is an act in which the highest degree of intimacy and emotional intensity is demanded, men and women are likely to reveal most sharply their basic ideas about themselves and their marital partners when they discuss sexual relations. It is also apparent in our data that many of the conflicts between husbands and wives are crystallized around sexual activity, and that attitudes on this subject often condense and bring into sharp focus broader attitudes toward marriage in general.

Individual feelings about sexual relations are extremely complex and often contradictory. Interview data of the kind collected in our study cannot be expected to capture the full complexity of the way respondents feel and behave sexually. The discussion which follows therefore will not be as complete as one might hope; a full exploration of sexual relations in working class marriages would require a much more intensive exploration of the subject than has been possible within the confines of a study devoted mainly to the investigation of family planning and contraception. However, it has been possible to collect data on the pattern of sexual relations in working class families and on the ways in which the sexual act is regarded by working class men and women. Perhaps our findings can serve to stimulate further research in this area, research which goes beyond the simple "outlet counting" of the Kinsey reports.

INITIATION AND MOTIVATION IN THE SEXUAL PARTNERSHIP

It is apparent in our data that most working class couples share certain cultural values concerning the appropriate roles of men and women in the sexual relationship. In general, men and women agree that the man is most fully sexual, that basically he is the one most interested in sexual activity. Even women who say that they enjoy intercourse often give the husband the edge in motivation for intercourse. It would seem that part of sexual etiquette in this group is to preserve the man's status as initiator and most interested party; his wife's role is that of either an interested or simply an accommodating partner.

As we will see, for some couples this is merely a bow to convention; in their day-to-day relations they may take considerable pride in the fact that both find deep gratification in their sexual relationship. At the same time, the pride and self-congratulation which some working class men show in being the more desirous partner suggests that this point of etiquette sometimes has deeper meaning and that some of these men would feel quite threatened if they believed that their wives' sexual interest proceeded independently of their own. As noted earlier, working class men do not feel in full control of their own lives; the sexual arena is one in which their culture supports their right to be in control, to have the main voice in deciding the way things are to go.

Most working class couples believe that the man is always satisfied in sexual intercourse, that the quality of his satisfaction does not vary in any important way from time to time. A few men and women comment that the husband enjoys intercourse most when his wife enjoys it most, but they are definitely in the minority. Male sexuality, then, is assumed to be rather simple, and ejaculation is taken to be synonymous with great pleasure. Women, on the other hand, are assumed to be much more variable in the extent to which they enjoy intercourse, if they enjoy it at all. This can be a source of envy and resentment on the part of wives because they feel that the husband has nothing to worry about in sexual relations; he is always satisfied, while her satisfaction depends upon her mood and her husband's patience and skill. At the same time, both husbands and wives feel that sexual gratification for the wife is much less important, so that, consciously at least, wives seem generally content if intercourse results in the husbands' pleasure even if not in their own. These couples see sex as primarily a male activity in initiation, interest, frequency of desire, and consistent gratification.

Only very occasionally in our data is the woman rather than the man regarded as the more "sexy." The few men who say that their wives' sexual interest is greater than their own do so ashamedly and defensively, typically blaming the demands of work for making them too tired to be interested. They also show considerable resentment about their wives' demands on them, as these interview quotations illustrate:

It's not important to me at all. Never did care for it to start with. I could take it or leave it, but not my wife, though; when she wants it she wants it.

They are most important to my wife. She's the one. I don't care about it or her when she nags, always after something.

The central threat these men feel is to their masculinity. Since they know that men are supposed to be more interested in sex, their wives' demands raise doubts about their own manliness. Regardless of their deeper needs, most of the men in our sample manage to behave in ways which maintain their sense of male control; the very few men in the group who do not are probably atypical in other ways as well. In any case, they serve to highlight the over-all pattern of male initiative among the working class couples we interviewed.

Since almost all the men in our sample indicate considerable enjoyment in sexual relations, the variation among women provides us with the simplest criterion for delineating different patterns among working class couples. Three broad categories are apparent in our data: (1) couples in which both husband and wife derive considerable gratification from their sexual relations, (2) couples in which the wife's enjoyment is subject to interference from other concerns and anxieties, and (3) couples in which the wife rejects sexual relations and in which intercourse is performed for the man's benefit, without the wife's deriving conscious gratification.

The first and last of these patterns reflect the two major tendencies, and both stand out quite sharply in our study. The second pattern represents an in-between category in which impulses both toward and against sexual enjoyment are operating. In many of these latter cases, problems of family planning and contraception are intimately related with the forces operating against a gratifying sexual relationship. In this chapter we will examine the two major categories, and we will defer to the following chapter, on the relationship between sexual behavior and family planning, a discussion of the in-between group.

PATTERNS OF MUTUALITY

Under this designation we will discuss those cases in which the couple, by husband's or wife's report, seem to approach the kind of sexual intimacy which can be said to constitute a healthy sexual adjustment in marriage and to approximate a "genital relationship," which Erikson (1950) describes as follows:

> Genitality, then, consists in the unobstructed capacity to develop an orgastic potency so free from pregenital [i.e., infantile sexual] interferences that genital libido (not just the sex products discharged in Kinsey's "outlets") is expressed in heterosexual mutuality, with full sensitivity of both penis and vagina, and with a convulsion-like discharge of tension from the whole body. . . . The total fact of finding, via the climactic turmoil of orgasm, a supreme experience of the mutual regulation of two human beings in some way breaks the point off the hostilities and potential rages caused by the oppositeness of male and female, of fact and fancy, of love and hate. Satisfactory sex relations thus make sex less obsessive, overcompensation less necessary, sadistic controls superfluous.

Erikson characterizes genitality defined in this manner as a "utopia," an ideal of perfection which healthy individuals may achieve but which is difficult to maintain consistently. He also notes that our culture seems to make consistent genital experience especially difficult.

Our data certainly do not allow us to test systematically for the full range of psychic experiences and meanings which genitality implies. However, the reports of some of our respondents suggest that they do approximate a mutual genital relationship in their marriages, and this is generally accompanied by a sense of satisfaction and security in the marriage greater than found among couples in the other two categories. This view is most eloquently expressed by one marginal upper-lower class woman with three children:

> Before I was married I was scared of sex. I thought it was a crime to do something like that. [Afterwards?] I found out that . . . let's put it this way, if God made anything better he kept it to himself. [Your sexual relationship?] It's wonderful; we both enjoy it. We do it at night when the children are sleeping; never during the day. We both come every time. It's the most important thing in the world. It just seems like we're happy all the time; it keeps us both happy. He feels the same way I do. He thinks it's the most important thing in the world, we both love it so. [Who enjoys it most?] We both enjoy it equal. [Orgasm?] Oh yes, uh huh, I have it, I have it every time! That's why I say it's wonderful.

This woman clearly cherishes sexual relations with her husband and finds in them the kind of "supreme experience" which, as Erikson notes, serves to erase the hostilities, rages, and sense of distance that are so easily built up when men and women live closely together in marriage.

As might be expected, those couples who find a great deal of pleasure in sexual relations tend to have intercourse more often. In our sample, over two-thirds of the husbands and wives who report mutual enjoyment indicate that they have intercourse more often than three times a week. Three-fourths of those who report ambivalence on the wife's part and eighteen of the nineteen cases in which the wife is reported to reject sexual relations indicate a frequency of less than three times a week. At least a third of these latter types speak of having intercourse only once a week. While it is certainly true that frequency is no simple index of sexual gratification, it also seems to be true that in the day-to-day lives of these couples frequency is determined by the degree of the wife's acceptance of sexuality; regardless of her husband's desires, she has ways of reducing the number of times they have relations if she does not desire them.

Two somewhat different orientations toward the mutual enjoyment of sex can be discerned. Some couples indicate a highly conscious orientation to the *sexual* quality of their relationships, they tend to think of themselves as "sexy" creatures, and to accept the natural "animal" quality that symbolically attaches to sexual relations in our culture. Other couples do not seem so consciously aware of these meanings and tend instead to emphasize a quieter, more interpersonal kind of enjoyment. They tend, perhaps, to suppress the more "sexy" notions out of some sense of propriety and fastidiousness. We shall call these two types "the sexy ones" and "the loving ones" to designate this different emphasis.

The Sexy Ones

One popular middle class stereotype of the lower class person is that he is highly sexed. Middle class people cherish a fantasy of the lower class as impulsive and freely self-indulgent because they are not hemmed in by prudery and constriction. This is more fantasy than fact, more wishfulness than reality. However, perhaps a third of the group do show some pleasurable identification with this kind of ideal; they do like to think of themselves and their spouses as "hot numbers." One lower-lower class father of five children, who has been married for twenty-four years, told the interviewer:

> When I was a kid I thought it was the greatest thing, and I still do. I get a big charge out of it, yeah man! We do it about four or five times a week; I'm cagier now than when I was twenty-five. [Cagier?] I do it more now than ever. [What is your wife's feeling?] Oh, she likes it too, and will give it to me any time I want it. We are having more intercourse now than when we were first married. I feel horny all the time. There ain't nothing no better. It gives me release. I'd like it more oftener, too. It means I got somebody to love. It couldn't be any better than it is. My wife enjoys it as much as me; she gets a thrill out of it as well as myself because she is just a sexy kind.

It is clear that this man is proud of his sexuality, particularly so because he is no longer a young man. He is also proud of his wife's being "a sexy kind," although we note that he still assumes his own priority as initiator (she gives "it" to him any time he wants).

Women, too, can speak pridefully of being sexy. Thus, a lower-lower class mother of three children, married for eight years, gave this description:

> Before we were married once I was necking in the car with my husband and I felt his thing. I asked him what that hard thing was and he said his flashlight, and I believed him. That's how dumb I was! He taught me everything I know and that's a lot. He is a great lover; it takes about two hours for us to have sex. Twice a week we have sex. It's slowed down because he works too hard. The first two years it was wonderful; now it's not too often.
>
> When he comes in the door he starts in on me. He loves me up and asks me if I'm going to be good to him tonight. It's usually always real crazy. He has me climbing the walls, and even if I'm not happy I put on a good act. When I'm tired it's no good, but I never let him know that; that's no good for his ego. When he plays around for an hour or so it's great. When it's a quickie it's not so good [for me]. He is always happy. I always tell him how handsome he is and that he is so big and strong. He brought home a French tickler once and it about drove me crazy. I don't like condoms anyway because I can't feel the sperm.

It is clear that this woman's pleasure comes partly from identifying with her husband and partly from the attention he pays to her via a long period of foreplay. It is also clear that "the climactic turmoil of orgasm" this woman seeks is achieved against inner obstacles that are overcome only with prolonged foreplay; but, in contrast with many other women in our sample, the important thing is that sexual pleasure is available to her.

A similar pattern of abandon is communicated by a lower-lower class mother of five children who has been married for sixteen years:

> I knew a little about sex when I got married. I learned quite a few different positions from my husband. I liked sex when I got

> married and I still do. It got better; it was good in the beginning, but since we talked to people and friends we got more good ideas. We have intercourse about four times a week. We just decide when we are in bed. He starts playing around and I get all excited. That's why I don't care what he uses [contraception] just so he keeps it up. I don't care what he uses just so he does it. I hate it when he stops, so sometimes he doesn't. We never get up during sex. I'm satisfied most of the time. I get all wet; I guess I come like a man does but only sometimes. When it's best I get crazy. It's almost always good except when I'm pregnant, sometimes it hurts, especially the last month. He always has a ball and always goes crazy.

In this case, interest in sexual abandon is such that contraception is regarded as a real interference and ignored some of the time. This woman looks to sex in desperation for some sense of pleasure and deep gratification (she was quoted in the previous chapter as saying, "My husband stinks"). She is more profoundly unhappy than the woman quoted above; for her, intercourse is a very necessary way of gaining some sense of aliveness and of pushing aside life's unpleasantness. The sexual relationship seems to be the only one in which she finds gratification with her husband.

An upper-lower class mother of three introduces a playfully seductive note in her story:

> I didn't know anything when I got married. My mother would have killed me; she'd have beat my head in. I've got a strict mother, you'd have to know her to appreciate her. Now we have it about four times a week. [How are you aware of your husband's desires?] All I have to do is just look at him. All I have to do is take it off. I always wear thin gowns, and I say, "Honey, tonight's the night." It's important to me; I don't get as nervous and tensed [when I have intercourse]. I think that's got a lot to do with women that are nervous. Hell, everybody else is going to the moon, I might as well go to heaven! It makes me feel I'm wanted, too. [Do you want intercourse more or less often?] I'll just take it any time I can get it; I like it. It reassures us of our love for each other. [How does your husband feel?] If I don't give it to him, you'd better believe he's mad the next day! It boosts his morale. All men feel that way; they think they are men then. My husband really enjoys it if I make it [have an orgasm]; he always waits for me.

The men and women who cherish an image of themselves as sexy together seem to value concretely and directly the orgastic experience—they use words like "crazy," "having a ball," "the thrill," to communicate the central gratification they find in sexual relations. The significance of the act lies very much in the physical pleasure they find and in the sense (which goes with giving full attention to the sexual experience) of having put aside worries and unpleasant concerns for a while. The women who indicate pleasure in their sexuality also betray some identification with their men—they are assertive in their desires for sexual gratification even though they are necessarily dependent on their husbands to provide the opportunity for it. They do not feel that they must be simply passive in order to be good women.

For both men and women, the sexual rites they perform together compensate effectively for some of the frustrations and uncertainties inherent in the working class world view. Their sexuality is an intimate oasis to which they can retreat from daily problems and in which they can find a renewed sense of aliveness and of support and closeness with another human being. Such, of course, is a function of intercourse in all social classes, but sexual relations acquire a particular significance in the contrast they provide with some of the less rewarding aspects of the working class world.

A concentration of attention on sexuality can, of course, be mixed with strong interpersonal values connected with intercourse. Our categories are based more on where emphasis lies than on exclusive involvement in the physical or the inter-personal aspects of sexual relations. Before discussing the latter as a major theme, therefore, we will quote extensively from an interview with an upper-lower class mother of two in which both themes are interwoven:

> I knew all about sex when I was about sixteen. I used to work in the dime store and there were a couple of girls who were married and they knew all about it and used to talk about it

all the time. Then I knew this friend who did it when she was going with some guy and she got caught. Then, you know, I did date a lot before I started to go with my husband and a lot of those guys tried to get fresh and tried to get you to do it. When I was going with my husband we used to neck a lot and he had a hard time holding it, and he even wanted to do it before we got married, and a couple of times we almost did, but I wouldn't let him even though I felt like it myself. But I figured we were going to get married soon anyway and we could wait and we wouldn't have to sneak it, and also I always used to think of my friend who got caught, and she was lucky the guy married her, and she was only seventeen years old. So I didn't want to get in trouble, and it's a good thing I didn't because something would have happened for sure, and everybody looks at you funny and calls you a bum.

When we were first married we used to do it only at night because we lived with my mother, and somebody was always at home. And anyway I used to work every day until I was in about my fourth month, I think. Then sometimes we would do it in the early morning, too, before we got up to go to work, and in the bedroom nobody would hear us. But most of the time we used to do it every night when we were first married. Now it got to be a little different because once in a while if my husband is delivering a car around lunch time, he comes home to eat, and if the kids are out or napping, or my older one goes to afternoon kindergarten, then he wants it sometimes after lunch. You know how these men are, if they want it, they want it. Sometimes I think my husband purposely comes home at lunch so he can have it. I always kid him and tell him he is going to wear it out. I tell him to save some of it for when he is older, but he is so strong he could do it five times a day.

I'll never forget when we were first married, he just couldn't get enough of it. We went to Starved Rock for our honeymoon, and I guess he was so anxious to do it because he waited so long and he would never touch another girl after he met me, and he didn't even go to a whorehouse after he met me; and that was kind of hard on him. So he was so excited that when we were in Starved Rock he just wanted to do it all day and all night long. Of course I think he would still do it like that. When we were there then we must have done it a hundred times.

[How about your desires now?] He never gives me a chance to have desires. He takes plenty good care of me. I always know he wants to do it, though. I don't know if he would be like that with anyone else if he wasn't married to me, but he is crazy about me. After the kids are sleeping and if the weather is bad and we go to bed early if there is nothing good on television, then we go to bed early so we can do it and not stay up too late, because he gets up at six o'clock, and sometimes the baby wakes up early so I have to get up before that. Usually he takes a bath before he goes to bed because he gets all greasy and sweaty from the gas station and I like it only if he is clean, so he takes a bath and I get in the bathroom first and I get into bed first and then he comes to bed and then we just start. I like it slow and he likes it fast because he would rather do it fast and do it again later like early in the morning, but lately I just like it slow and just once.

[How does your sexual satisfaction vary from time to time?] Well, I usually like it, but I don't like it twice in one time during the night and the morning too. It's too much. I don't always get satisfied and my husband does, but I let him do it anyway. He always feels better when he does it. I like it best right after my period because then I haven't had it for a few days and it's like starting fresh all over again. Sometimes I like it if my husband wakes me up after he takes his shower. Sometimes I fall asleep while I am waiting for him, and then I like it real lots. [What determines the variation?] Oh, it depends I guess on how I feel, if I'm not too tired; and sometimes if my husband goes too fast then I don't like it so much either. And if he doesn't take a shower and if he is all sweaty then I don't like it so much.

[What about his satisfaction?] Oh, gosh, he is always satisfied. I never knew a time when he didn't get satisfied. I wish I could be as satisfied as that guy is. He would rather do that than eat, and he is a good eater, too.

The Loving Ones

These men and women emphasize the non-physical aspects of intercourse and its aftereffects more than the orgastic gratifications. This does not mean that the latter are not at the core of the experience, but these individuals are more concerned with (and perhaps feel more comfortable thinking about) the less directly sexual aspects. For example, one lower-lower class mother of one child speak in this vein:

> I didn't know anything about sex before I got married. I knew about how babies came and I had an idea how they were born, but I had just heard little bits of my mother's friends talking about it before I left the room. I was scared; I thought it was sinful. [What about your relations now?] We have it three or four times a week. I'm very aware of his desires; I can always tell what's on his mind. He always tries to please me and see that I'm satisfied, too. We do it about as often as when we were married and I enjoy it more. It's real important to me; it makes me feel good and assures me of his love. It's just as important for him as me. We just enjoy it; it's something very beautiful to both of us. We talk about it a lot, but I just can't tell you the things we say about our lovin'.

Individual gratification is important for this woman, but her emphasis is on quieter qualities; sexual relations assure her of her husband's love and are a "very beautiful" experience.

An upper-lower class father of a four-month-old child, married for three years, was more specific in speaking of the functions of sexual relations for him:

> I'd say it's a pretty pleasant experience. We usually do it at night or sometimes in the morning or just about when we feel like doing it; we have even done it in the afternoon. We average about twice a week, I guess. My wife always seems ready and willing when I'm ready. We don't do it as much now as we used to; when we were first married we did it every night for a while. It's pretty important to me; it brings you and your wife closer—and I don't mean what you're thinking! We get along better. It makes me feel pretty good, but tired after. It's important to her, too, she's always nicer to me after. She is more contented and she acts nicer. We both like it, and I think she feels she is pleasing me also. We generally get along better for a few days.

This man is highly conscious of the day-to-day interpersonal gains from making love to his wife; intercourse is instrumental for him—it makes him tired (so he sleeps soundly), it makes his wife nicer to him, it brings them closer to each other, etc. For these people the sexual relationship is very closely linked with other aspects of their family relationship, as one lower-lower class mother of two young children makes clear:

> I didn't know much about sex before I got married. I didn't think much about it because I was so much in love. I was a little scared, too. [Now?] It's just about like it was when we first got married. Anytime he wants me for a wife, it's O.K. with me. That's the way it should be. If you want to have a happy family you have to feel that way about each other. It's important to both of us; it makes us feel closer to each other. We both enjoy it equally.

This woman brings the sexual relationship into the family relationship in a very solid way and regards it as a binding force. As such, it serves to strengthen the marriage by making the tie between husband and wife more intimate and happier. It is in this context, rather than as a separate goal, that the orgastic experience achieves significance. Another woman, an upper-lower class mother of five children said:

> I didn't know *anything* about sexual relations before I was married. I was green as grass. We do it about three or four times a week, night or day; it just happens, we don't plan it. It's another way of expressing how much we love each other. It makes me feel . . . I just enjoy it. It's just as important to me as to him. He sees to it that I have a climax every time.

Achieving sexual gratification together seems a source of real pride and satisfaction to this group, just as it is to the group that highlights sexual experience as such. Finding gratification requires that the husband be solicitous of his wife's state of mind, and the loving attention that this implies is gratifying to the wife on non-sexual grounds as well. An upper-lower class mother of two reflects this dependence on her husband for solicitude in sexual relations when she says:

> I knew what married people did before I was married, but I had no experience. I learned it's something pretty wonderful —I learned from my husband, of course. I was a little afraid when I got married but I soon felt differently. The longer we are married the better it seems. The first year we were both young and didn't know too much, but now he knows what I like and what makes me happy. It took a few years to adjust. We do it about once a week. We can usually tell when we kiss each other goodnight.

> I guess our relationship is about average. I would say we are a typical couple and we are happy. Most of the time I'm satisfied. When we have sex and it's good I feel very good, but when it's quick I'm not happy and it's hard for me to fall asleep. When it's best I'm very relaxed and happy. If it's real fast, I'm disgusted. I feel very let down. If my husband takes his time and kisses me and so on, I feel good and love him very much and I really feel he loves me. He's always satisfied whether it's fast or takes time. I think men are always happy. He is really most satisfied when I am, though.

The fundamental attitude of these wives toward intercourse is that a dutiful wife must participate to gratify her husband. No one mentions a similar duty of the husband to his wife; it is assumed that he is always interested in sexual relations and therefore the question of duty is not relevant. Since they are duty-bound to participate, and since they are aware that their own gratification is not automatic, these wives show a strong sense of gratitude to husbands with whom they find enjoyment in sexual relations, an enjoyment which for this group is intimately bound up with the sense of closeness intercourse gives them.

An upper-lower class mother of two children shows her consciousness of the priority of duty when she says:

> My husband taught me all I know about sex; maybe that's why we enjoy each other so much. The way he explained it to me was that that was what marriage was for, and I just accepted it as part of my duty as a wife—I really shouldn't say duty because I enjoy it as much as he does, I think.
>
> We usually do it about four times during the week, and two or three times on the weekend. During the week it's usually when we go to bed and at any time on weekends. We are very aware and considerate of each other. [Has it changed since you were first married?] No, I wouldn't say so except maybe to the extent that he didn't work steady then and we had more free time and it was a good pastime.
>
> It's very important to me—I'm sure it releases some pent-up tensions. I usually feel relaxed. It has about the same effect on him. He gets a little disgruntled; you can tell it on him if it's too long between times. I also think they draw a couple closer together; it gives you a deeper feeling for each other.

It is clear that the wife's sexual duty can be regarded as a pleasant one. Often wives have some difficulty in resolving the demands of this pleasant duty with their responsibilities as mothers, but where a desire for a good sexual relationship is present, they are able to do so. For example, one mother of three told the interviewer:

> I knew very little about sex when I got married. You know how kids talk; most of it is guesswork and imagination. My husband explained it all to me so clearly and simply. I felt it was part of getting married, that it was just supposed to be, that's all. I looked forward to it. [Now?] I want to satisfy him fully, and I believe I do. [How often?] We take two or three during the week and at least three on weekends. Since the children are here, I find it a little hard to always avail myself every time he would like me to. He works the second shift and I'm asleep when he comes home, and many times in the morning the children are up and around.
>
> [Your feelings] I feel that it is part of life. We were meant to have it and it brings us closer together. It reassures me that my husband loves me and wants me near him. [How do you feel about frequency?] I'd say five or six times a week is sufficient; anything can be overdone. [What are your husband's feelings about it?] It is very important to him. He gets grumpy and irritable if it's very long, more than a day between. I guess it gives him an emotional outlet. He enjoys it more, I'd say. I enjoy it, but I don't feel it is a necessity to life like he does.

This woman does not really like to think of herself as "sexy"; to some extent she conceals from herself her autonomous sexual interests. However, because she accepts her duty and wants very much to make her husband happy, she is able to find pleasure in sexual relations and to achieve a measure of mutuality in her relationship with him. Other women with similar problems of sleeping schedules and children use the situation as an excuse to avoid love-making. A woman such as this, who is able to believe that sex is a force for solidifying the marital relationship and whose husband also wants sex to be a mutual pleasure and dissolver of hostility (he gets "grumpy" if they do not have intercourse often), recognizes the threat that such an excuse represents to her family relationships.

The respondents who communicate some sense of mutuality in their sexual relationship, whether it be of the sexual or of the loving variety, are those who also find their family life generally satisfying. The wives in both groups, for example, do not complain of their husbands' drinking and (with one exception) speak of them as good husbands and "wonderful" in their relations with the children. Their descriptions sound like this:

Women of the sexy type:

> I have a fine husband; he's a swell guy. He works very hard and I am very proud of him.
> We get along wonderful. He loves the children. He's gentle, a good father, a very nice personality.
> He is real cute, tall and strong. We get along real good. He's a swell guy.
> He's quiet, well pleased by his family. He's a home man. He works hard. He has a small garage and I tell you, I'd rather have him under a auto body than on top of another body like my first husband. He brings me flowers. He shows us a good example by listening to us when it's necessary; regardless of what's important to him he listens to what we have to say.

Women of the loving type:

> He has an unusually good disposition. He's handsome. He spends his time off from work at home and with us, his family.
> He's a good father and husband. He loves to play with the children. We get along fine; we are very happy.
> He's always nice to everyone and aware of their feelings. He's kind and gentle, and he'd give you the shirt off his back.
> He's good, kind, and considerate. He doesn't drink.
> He doesn't drink; he doesn't swear. He's a wonderful father and husband. He stays with the kids or he helps me at home.
> He's a good worker. He loves the boys. We get along fine. The kids cry to go with him every time he goes out.
> He has a nice personality and makes friends easily. He's good to the children and takes care of them when I'm gone.

Mutuality in sex, then, seems to go with a kind of family life not easily achieved in the working class, and with a style of family living that many working class wives wish for but do not achieve. We will see later that part of their failures may lie in a rejection of their roles as sexual partners. For men, failure may result from their not giving their wives the kind of attention in sexual relations that are so meaningful in non-sexual ways as well. While working class men and women agree that sex is *primarily* for the husband, some husbands seem to believe that this pleasure is *exclusively* for them. Others seem to find increased satisfaction, both sexual and non-sexual, from their wives' psychic participation in sexual relations. It is understandable that such an attitude should go with a general desire to share and participate intimately with the family which together they create.

PATTERNS OF REJECTION

Many working class women reject sexuality as a meaningful and gratifying activity. Their husbands seldom express a lack of interest in sexual relations, but it is clear that some husbands reject mutuality; they regard intercourse as very much their own pleasure and their wives are seen merely as servants of their desires. In these relationships, there is no hint of genital mutuality; responses range from cases in which the woman rejects sexuality as disgusting to those in which she tries to accept sexuality as her duty and denies any feeling, positive or negative. These couples seldom say they have intercourse as often as three times a week; in about half the cases it occurs once a week or less, and because there is seldom mutual desire and interest, its frequency may vary widely from time to time. Thus one mother of three children, who is intimidated and perplexed by sexuality even after four years of marriage, told the interviewer:

Before we were married I was pregnant, but I still didn't know nothing about it. I knew I had had the intercourse but I didn't know what it was all about. It was on his birthday and he was drinking, and we went to his house and no one was there and we went on his bed and it happened. [Did you know this was intercourse?] Yes, I guess I did. We were just kissing and it happened. I wasn't scared but I knew I shouldn't have done it, and I was scared about his mom seeing the blood all over the bed. I guess I learned everything I know about it right then. I enjoyed it but I don't know what I felt about it. I thought it was what I had heard people whispering about, and I liked sharing the secret.

[Now?] My husband likes it right before he goes to sleep. Sometimes he wants it every night and sometimes three or four weeks go by when he's not bothering me. I could do without it. I never have said no; but I'm afraid he'd go somewhere else. [Is he aware of your feelings?] No, I always act interested; I don't know how he could know. It's not important to me; it don't do nothing for me. He could do without it for my part. I don't know how important it is to him. [Do you discuss it?] No, he don't talk much; he don't ever talk about it. Sometimes I'd like to, but once or twice I tried and he acted like he was deaf. I know he talks to his friends about it, but not to me.

Clearly "it" still happens *to* this woman; she has no sense of participation in the sexual act by her own wish. Yet she feels duty-bound to participate if she is to keep her husband. For his part, he has no interest in discussing the matter; he prefers to take it when he wants it and not have to worry about her feelings or desires. Although she has some vague notion that a woman might enjoy intercourse too, she has never had a chance to move in that direction because of her husband's attitude. The educational role of the husband, which is so apparent in the cases of mutual participation, is manifested here in a negative way. Whereas for the first group of couples, the wives feel that their husbands have guided them toward mutual enjoyment, these women feel that their husbands have educated them only in the bare essentials necessary to perform the act. It is about such couples as these that Nathan Ackerman (1958) has remarked:

> Sex tends sometimes to become mechanized and depersonalized, a physical release that leaves the partners even lonelier after

the act than before. The expression of tender sentiment shrinks. Sex becomes the arena for the struggle for dominance and control. Or it becomes a drab, hollow routine, carried out on schedule. . . . Sometimes sex simply dies a slow, withering death.

Among our respondents, the men who do not speak of mutual enjoyment tend to be highly evasive. Often it seems that they have never really thought about how their wives feel; they conceive of intercourse only as something they do every once in a while to make themselves feel better. Often these men will say that they "knew all about sex" before they were married, but their comments suggest that they knew only that men engage in such an activity and that they are supposed to enjoy it. For example, one father of four children has this to say about sexual relations after sixteen years of marriage:

I knowed all about it before I got married through friends that I went to school with and things like that. [Now?] It's like it always was; we do it maybe once a week or more or less often, sometimes twice a month. [What are your wife's desires?] I don't know how to answer that. [Is she aware of your desires?] She's aware, I guess. [How have things changed?] Since the children have come along, a lot of changes. I don't know how to put it . . . we can't get together too much any more. Some of the reason is that she's tired from the kids, and a lot of the time I'm tired because of my work. I lift over twenty tons a day twice. That's forty tons! We figures it out once, a buddy and me.

[What is the importance of sex to you?] Well, it's just as important as anything else; that's not the answer you want, but, well, that's it. I think I'm missing something. [How does your wife feel about it?] She's not too sexually . . . you know. I don't know what it does for her. [To whom it is more important?] I don't know, me I guess. I think you have to get rid of that sperm or whatchacallit for health's sake as well as enjoyment. [Does your wife enjoy it at all?] She gets satisfaction, doesn't she? Like I say, I can probably feel for me and can tell you how I feel [but not how she feels].

For many of these men, sex comes to mean simply something one does for "health's sake." Over the years, the positive pleasures of intercourse disappear for them and they are reduced to thinking of sexual relations simply in an eliminative way; one has to get rid of "that sperm" juts as one must urinate and defecate. Where this is the dominant conception of intercourse, it is not surprising that the wife feels rejected and unwilling to participate with interest. When sex is viewed in this basically hostile way, it is understandable that sexual relations are relatively infrequent after the early period of marriage and that intercourse occurs only when the pressure of instinctual forces has built up strongly.

The interpersonal frictions surrounding the activity are likely to make it seem tiresome, as some of our respondents comment. One father of five children, married for nineteen years, spoke of sexual relations in the following way:

> I learned about sex when I was eighteen. Other guys told me about it. Once I went to prove it to myself, to a prostitute. But I thought the best thing was to get married. Those kind of women [prostitutes], they go with all different men. With your own wife, you know it's safe. [How does your wife feel about it?] Sometimes she's interested, but when people are young they like it very much; when they go together for a long time they don't love it so much. We have it once in a while, that's enough. Afterwards I'm tired as hell. She don't like it too much. She gets tired, too.

The sense of effort comes through directly here. While men for whom sex is more of a mutual pleasure also may mention the interference of work fatigue, it appears that the more hostile men find such interference much greater, since they cannot look to sexual relations for the same sense of replenishment. They tend to think of intercourse merely as a strenuous activity which expels physical products that must be gotten out of the system.

Among women who reject sexuality, we find two major emphases: some sharply reject sexual activity and clearly indicate that they would prefer never to have intercourse; others defend themselves in a different way by seeking to make the issue of sexual relations as unemotional as possible. These latter women say that they do not feel either happy or unhappy about having to engage in the activity as long as it is not too frequent.

The Active Rejecters

These women seem the most unhappy about sexual relations. They react with conscious or implicit disgust, fear or anxiety, and they find it difficult to understand why fate so unkindly requires women to participate in an unpleasant activity. One mother of three children, married for twelve years, said:

> I knew very little. I knew where babies came from and how you got that way. Actually, the first time I saw a condom I couldn't understand how the man could get that little thing on. I really never thought much about it. I knew it's something you did. I think it's something you expect in marriage. [Now?] We don't do it much, about once a week; sometimes twice if I can't talk him out of it or make him mad enough. I guess it's a heck of a life for a man. [Are you aware of his desires?] I can tell, believe me! No matter what you do, it's all right, and he's very sweet.
> From what I hear from girl friends, they are all like that. It's terrible to say, but it's not important to me at all. I don't feel anything. You'll think I'm lying but I'm not. I could read a magazine. It disgusts me or makes me mad. He says it makes him feel very good; he gets depressed otherwise. [Who is it most important to?] Guess who, him! I'm sure of that because I don't enjoy it at all.

This woman's rejection is quite active, perhaps because she fears that if she were to enjoy sex she would be a bad woman. She does get some aggressive pleasure from sexual relations, however, in her opportunity to frustrate and anger her husband.

A woman who has been married for nineteen years and has three children tells a similar story of frigidity:

> I didn't know anything when I was married. My husband told me some on our wedding night; I had never heard it discussed

before. I guess I thought it was my duty, and I have felt that way ever since—when he wants me I'm to let him have me. [Now?] I'd say we do it two or three times a week. I'm sure I'd never have to have a man, but he feels it's a necessary part of his life— he's always been a hot number. I'd never have to have it; it does nothing for me except disgust me when he's drinking and keeps pestering me. I have no idea what it does for him except he's still a young man. [What do you mean?] If he can come several times a week, he's still young. I don't believe either one has to have it to live a normal life. He calls it pleasure, but I'd rather be with friends on a picnic or something for my pleasure.

This woman has her feelings more under control than the first, but she still feels disgust and insult in her sexual role. She has some underlying admiration of her husband as a young "hot number," but this seems only to make intercourse a little less intolerable.

Most of the women who actively reject sexuality are not so forthright about their rejection, but they are nevertheless assiduous in avoiding intercourse when they can. Some are aware that they really should not feel the way they do; for example, one mother of three, who has been married for fifteen years, said:

[How did you learn about sex?] I didn't learn nothing. I was told about menstruation when it happened. My foster mother told me that it would happen every month and that I'd have to wear a pad; that's all she ever said. I read a lot about it in my sister-in-law's [nursing] books, and while we were engaged we talked about what I was reading. I was scared to go home with him. He was very understanding and assured me everything would be all right. [Now?] It isn't too often, only about every two or three weeks.

I don't enjoy it because I heard nothing but filth about it when I was young. It's hard for me. I can't relax. I know it isn't sinful, but I remember the bad things I heard. My husband is understanding. [How do you know his desires?] I can tell as soon as he walks in the door when he wants it. They always pat you on the tail, and he wouldn't argue about anything when he wants it.

[What are the changes since you were married?] I'm a little more relaxed; I still don't want it, but I know it's my duty. He doesn't try too often because he understands. I could always live without it; I just don't need it. If I could just relax it might be better. My husband is very understanding about sex; he holds his urge back for my benefit. He does it because he enjoys it; I do it because it's my duty. If I had to do it for a living, I'd starve.

Yet apparently this woman feels that she does "do it for a living," in the sense that sexual intercourse is one of the things required of her as a wife. She cannot seem to separate in her mind the prostitute's degradation and her own proper role in marriage. Such attitudes probably underly much of what women of this type say, but few state them so openly. Also, this woman accepts the situation as arising from her own feelings and does not blame her husband; more often, such women blame their husbands for desires that seem senseless or hostile to them. Thus, one woman who has been married for nine years expressed her feelings about sex as follows:

> All my mother ever taught me was not to let boys get anywhere with me. She didn't explain nothing; she told me not to let no boys be loving over me. She told me when I was about twelve; I didn't even know what she meant. I guess she meant if they loved all over you what it would cause. [Now?] We do it two or three times a week. [What are his desires?] We're generally at home and I don't know how he feels except his loving right over me. It don't make me no difference. I'd like it less often, but you have to do it if you live with a man whether you're for it or against it. It's not so good for me; most of the time I'd rather not. [What does sex do for him?] I don't know. I just don't know. He enjoys it the most. I don't never have no chance to want to, I don't guess, because *they* always want to all the time, they don't give *you* a chance to want it!

This woman is still a prisoner of the point of view her mother communicated to her, and she is unable to break out because her husband seems to her like all the other boys her mother told her about. It is interesting that several women in this category, in referring to their husbands, shift from the singular pronoun "him" to the plural "they" when speaking of sexual relations. Their distrustful attitudes toward men come especially to the fore in discussing sex. A complaint that the husband never waits for his wife's desires is not uncommon, but one gets the impression that the husband who is willing to wait would wait a very long time. At the same time, it is also clear that the husbands, perhaps perplexed at their wives' resistance, take the attitude that coitus is something they have coming to them regardless of how their wives feel.

The wife often feels disdain for the husband who demands such an inexplicable pleasure. Over a period of time, she may become used to his "peculiarity," but she still basically rejects sexual relations. Thus one mother of five, married for fifteen years, gave this resigned view:

> I knew from my older sister that a woman and a man were supposed to have relations of that kind after they were married. She told me those things after my mother died, before I was married. I really can't say I thought too much about it one way or the other. I didn't fear it and I didn't look forward to it. [Now?] Our sexual relations are the same now as they were when we were first married. It's still done just for him, only whenever he feels he wants it. The only difference now is that he is away all week and is home only on weekends so we can't have relations more than two or three times a week. When he was home all the time, it was about every other night.
>
> I am quite aware of his desires; I couldn't help but be. He lets me know right away when he gets home. He is aware of my desires to the extent that he knows I would prefer not to do it at all. Sexual relations are not in the least important to me. They do nothing at all for me. I do it because I feel it's my duty and that's all. I would prefer it much less often myself because to me it's only a bother and a worry and an unpleasant duty. I don't know that there is any way it would be better for me unless it would be not to have any at all. [What about his interest?] It seems to be quite important to him; you would think he couldn't live without it. They must give him a lot of satisfaction, relief or something, because he sure likes it. I don't know why he feels that way, I just don't. He gets a lot of pleasure and enjoyment from it, I guess. I get no feeling one way or the other.

This woman would like to feel that she has no trouble in tolerating sexual relations. However, her underlying

attitude is made quite clear in the story she tells about a picture showing a man and a woman who, she was told, "are talking about a problem in their sexual relationship." She completed the story in this way:

> I think he is asking her why she is so cold toward him. She is thinking that she just wishes he would leave her alone, she is so disgusted because she has to do that and then worry herself sick about being pregnant.

She is not able to bring about any real compromise between her underlying sense of disgust and her husband's desires for intercourse, even after fifteen years of marriage.

The result in such cases is a sense of entrenched conflict. Thus, one mother of four children, who has been married for seventeen years, uses a variety of techniques to avoid her husband:

> We do not take many chances because I am not strong. My husband wants it; he's like all men. At first it was almost every night and later it was when he got the chance when the children were not around. Now the kids might not be here but he knows how I feel. Sometimes he argues and sometimes he just goes out and gets a beer. I let him have his way often enough, maybe two or three times a month. Of course, I was sick with flu for the last six weeks and he never bothered me. I am glad my husband comes home, some don't, but it is not good for me. I do not feel excited about him like that very much.
>
> All men need to more than the women. They get relief and a woman hardly ever needs relief. I remember when we were first married sometimes I wanted him to, but after seventeen years of marriage, well, we just don't need to, that's all. I think it makes a man feel young. You know, they still look the girls over when they have grown daughters of their own. [Who enjoys it most?] The man, every time. That's nature. It is important to them to be a man with women. With me, it's not so important. I raised my family and was a good wife. At first, in the good times, we had pleasure. I still go along but it is not the same with the woman.

Apparently, youth was this woman's only excuse for enjoying sexuality; having settled down as a family woman, sex no longer has meaning to her. Sickness can be used as an excuse, and she feels justified in refusing her husband because she no longer has sexual needs, although she knows that he still needs "relief." Other women of this type tell us that they go out into the street to let the husband cool off when he makes advances, or that they "get the children around so he can't get close to me." In this way their relationship becomes a battleground of chronic disagreement between the husband, who demands his right for eliminative relief, and the wife, who resents demands that she participate in a disgusting and meaningless act.

The Repressive Compromisers

While their basic attitudes toward sexual relations are not really different, another group of women seek to neutralize their negative feelings and to regard their wifely duty as simply another chore. Although they are never completely successful in thus damping their affective response, they are often able to work out with their husbands a compromise that allows them to avoid so consistent a sense of conflict. These women try to be unfeeling in serving their husbands; in return, they usually expect that the men will moderate their desires considerably. Thus a mother of three who has been married for seventeen years gave this picture:

> I didn't really know anything much about sex. I knew there was relations, but I didn't know the satisfactions that a husband and wife should have. My husband was considerate of that, and he took it upon himself to first consider me. [Now?] I get along very well on that. We don't even argue about it. We started out not arguing or disagreeing about it. Actually, things haven't changed much. We both think it is important if we want to stay happy. I don't think a woman cares much for it, but she knows a man does and she should try to keep a man satisfied. I could do with less; it's too much trouble and I wouldn't want to if it didn't please him. I think it's very important to him. It makes a man think that you really do love him and you think of him. I think a woman can love a man and not have sex relations, but a man can't, it seems. We just don't get much pleasure out of it and we don't want to be bothered.

This woman recognizes the potentiality for disagreement about sex, but she has done her best to minimize this by (as she thinks) meeting her husband halfway. In return, she has apparently been able to persuade him not to make more demands than she is willing to tolerate.

The sense of distance from sexual participation felt by these women is clearly communicated by another woman, married for thirteen years, for whom sexual relations seem to "just happen";

> I didn't know anything. It's awful to be that dumb, but my mother never did teach us anything like that. I didn't even realize how a woman could get pregnant. After I was married my husband told me I would probably get pregnant. [How did you feel about sex then?] I guess I didn't feel any way about it, not knowing what it was all about. I just figured my husband would take care of everything, and he did. [Now?] Well, it happens about a couple of times a week. After you live with a man over thirteen years you usually can tell when he wants it. I'm satisfied the way things are. I don't dread it and I don't look forward to it. I think there would be more pleasure in it if it didn't happen too often. I don't know why, I just do. [How does your husband feel?] Well, he likes it, but it's not all he lives for, I guess, because he's the considerate kind. I guess it just gives him the feeling of being married. [Why?] Because he loves me, I guess.

In a somewhat motherly way, this woman encourages her husband to regard sex as unimportant without arguing with him about it. She seeks to make the activity a relatively empty expression of asexual affection—something that is really unimportant but that men feel they must do from time to time. By not confronting herself with the genital significance of sexual relations, she is able to repress her underlying negative feelings and maintain the view that "sex is no trouble for me."

Many women seek this kind of repressive compromise, but only a few manage to attain stability in it. The few who do probably succeed because their husbands are cooperative and because the couple fix their attention on other goals in marriage, in ways that allow them to minimize the importance of their differing attitude toward sexual relations. Over a period of time, such women probably manage to persuade their husbands that sex is really not so important. Both the active rejecters and the repressive compromisers feel duty-bound to be sexual partners: the former are not able to master their sense of unpleasantness and fear about sexuality; the latter are able to do so by strict denial of these negative feelings.

As might be expected, these patterns of rejection are related to one or another disturbance of closeness and intimacy in the marital relationship generally. In contrast to those respondents who share a mutual genital relationship, the rejecters show much less enthusiasm in describing their spouses. Whereas the women in the first category tended to speak of their husbands as "fine," "swell," "nice to everyone," the latter women either are directly critical or indicate some sense of distance in their descriptions.

The active rejecters, of course, reflect the poorest image of their husbands. A majority complain of drinking: one woman says her husband threatens to kill her when he is drunk, another that he is rough and loud, another that he drinks in solitary fashion and goes to sleep. Similarly, they speak of their husbands as cross, as too lenient with the children, as sloppy about moral standards, as staying away from home too much, etc. Clearly the sexual difficulty is part of an over-all pattern in which the woman feels herself one of her husband's minor pleasurable pursuits, and not infrequently she also feels that he is dangerously aggressive in his attitudes toward her.

The repressive compromisers do not have these troubles. Just as they are inclined to describe their husbands as sexually considerate, they tend to speak of them as considerate in other areas. However, their descriptions concentrate on negative virtues—"he doesn't drink" or "he doesn't gamble," "we've never had a bad argument"—rather than on more positive values. The admiring affection reflected by many of the women who show mutuality in sexual relations is conspicuously absent.

THE PREVALENCE OF MUTUALITY AND REJECTION

These two patterns are complex, and they certainly overlap. Some women who fit the mutuality pattern do so only against underlying anxieties about their sexual behavior. Some women who fit the rejection pattern are there despite their wish that they could be more "relaxed" in sexual relations. However, the dominance of one or the other tendency is clear in most of the respondents. A third group which, because of its particular relevance to problems of family planning and contraception, will be considered in the next chapter, falls between these two extremes. These are women who recognize in themselves some interest and gratification in sexual relations but who are unable to participate without mixed feelings because of their anxieties.

On the whole, not quite half our sample seems to conform to the mutuality pattern, somewhat less than a third to the rejection pattern, and about the same number to the in-between category. In general, mutuality seems more characteristic of the upper-lower class than of the lower-lower—as one would expect, given the generally less distant relationship between upper-lower class wives and husbands and the sense of strain and conflict so common among lower-lower class couples. In our sample, about three-fourths of the upper-lower class women indicate some measure of mutual enjoyment in their discussions of sexual relations, compared to about one-fourth of the lower-lower class women. On the other hand, about 40 per cent of the lower-lower class women indicate a real rejection of sexuality, compared with only 10 per cent of the upper-lower class women. More lower-lower class women are in the in-between category, principally because of their concern over becoming pregnant.

chapter vii

SEXUAL RELATIONS, FAMILY PLANNING, AND CONTRACEPTION

THE RELATIONSHIP between sexual attitudes and ways of handling family planning and contraception is complex; nevertheless, the pattern of sexual relations does seem to influence contraceptive behavior strongly and in a number of different ways. Because of the close association between attitudes toward sexual relations and attitudes toward one's spouse, both directly affect the couple's degree of co-operation in formulating and carrying out family planning goals. In addition, particular attitudes toward intercourse and toward genitalia strongly influence contraceptive practice, both as to the method chosen and the regularity with which it is used. We will examine family planning and contraceptive activity for each of the two sexual patterns discussed thus far, and then examine some of the effects on sexual relations of a fear of pregnancy because of ineffective contraception.

GENITAL MUTUALITY AND CONTRACEPTION

In general, those couples who experience mutuality in their sexual relationship are satisfied with their family planning. As might be expected, the sense of personal closeness and co-operation that goes with genital mutuality carries with it an openness in the discussion of family planning goals and effective co-operation in some method of contraception. In our sample, almost three-fourths of the women who are effective at contraception show some striving toward mutuality; a few do so against significant psychic obstacles, but most seem quite satisfied with their sexual adjustment. In contrast, only slightly over one-third of the ineffective women share mutual pleasure in sexual relations with their husbands.

Furthermore, most of the ineffective couples in the mutuality group have not yet reached the family size they wish. As noted earlier, few working class couples begin contraception in earnest until they are close to having the number of children they want. Thus, those ineffective couples who share a mutual relationship include several who see no vital reason to practice contraception until some time in the future. With one exception (the woman quoted in the previous chapter whose mutual sexual pleasure with her husband is almost the only source of gratification in her relationship with him), there are no cases of sporadic or careless ineffective contraceptive users in their group. Either the couple does not use contraception at all because they are willing to have more children or they do use contraception in regular and effective ways.

It is understandable that acceptance of sexuality makes it easier for a couple to address itself concretely to the issue of contraception. For these couples, there is a minimum of interference from attitudes of sexual avoidance and guilt. It is possible for them to be rational and direct in dealing with the genital issues connected with day-to-day contraceptive practice. This is apparent in the matter-of-fact way effective women of this type respond when asked whether their contraceptive method interferes with sexual relations. Typical responses are along this line:

> It works out fine. It's just a little trouble to stop and put it [diaphragm] in. It's a little trouble to get up, but it's easier than having a baby.

> We go to bed and if we decide to have sex, then just before something happens, I get up and insert it [diaphragm].
>
> When we are ready to do it and he gets ready to stick it in, then he puts the rubber on, but he doesn't have to get out of bed because it's under the pillow; he does it so quick, he's got so much experience already he can do it in the dark without looking.

Because the activity itself is pleasant and because these couples feel relatively secure in their sexual relationship, they are better able to tolerate the minor inconveniences connected with contraception.

As to particular contraceptive methods, we find that those women who enjoy their sexual relationships accept feminine methods more readily than do the others. A majority use feminine methods (diaphragm, suppository, jelly, tablet). Others who are now ineffective or whose husbands use condoms express an interest in some feminine method, usually the diaphragm. Thus, one woman, whose doctor had told her she was sterile after her third child but who later became pregnant, told the interviewer:

> After the baby is born I'm going to talk to my doctor about not having any more children. My religion is against prevention, but I can't afford to feel that way. The diaphragm is about the soundest way, I think. I've heard of a number of cases where it worked.

Another woman, whose husband now uses condoms, would like to have a diaphragm if she can overcome her embarrassment about asking her physician.

These women are more likely to accept the responsibility for contraception, regardless of the method used. Often they feel that both husband and wife should take responsibility, but just as often they feel that the woman should be more responsible because she must bear and care for the children. These are common responses to the question among this group of women:

> Either one [should be responsible] that it is most convenient for. I don't think it is up to the husband any more

than the wife. After all, women get the satisfaction as much as the men.

The wife should be responsible for it. It's the wife's job because there are so many ways she can use but a husband has rubbers or nothing. I have heard that rubbers are not too safe anyway.

I think both the husband and wife should share the responsibility. They are the parents, they are the ones who will either enjoy the relationship or fight over it. Both are responsible.

Both I'd say. I think any two married people should make their decisions together.

This kind of attitude holds equally for couples who are and are not now contraceptive users; the ineffective women believe that contraception would be their responsibility should they decide to limit the number of children they have.

It is interesting to note that all the ineffective women in our sample who display the mutuality pattern are Catholic. Perhaps this, too, plays a part in their failure to take up contraception; so long as their families are not larger than they want, their religious views are not tested by excess fertility. One of these women did use a diaphragm in her first marriage (to a man with whom she did not get along) and does not use contraception now because she is starting a second family; another ineffective woman douches only for cleanliness and has had three nicely spaced children in ten years of marriage. In one way or another, then, those couples who share a mutually gratifying sexual relationship have managed to avoid having more children than they want. As we shall see, where this is not the case a severe strain is put on the woman's sexual adjustment.

SEXUAL REJECTION AND CONTRACEPTION

Among those couples where the wife actively rejects sexuality, very few are effective contraceptive users, and about one-third of the ineffective users fall into this category. Furthermore, the effective ones in this group tend to be late planners who have taken up contraception in desperation after having as many or more children than they really want. As might be expected, contraception tends to be an issue of conflict for these couples, and the wife's rejection of sexuality, coupled as it often is with the husband's hostile, eliminative ideas about intercourse, makes smooth contraceptive performance particularly difficult.

The few effective couples in this actively-rejecting group all use condoms, and both the husbands and the wives consider contraception the husband's responsibility. The wives' rejection of sexuality often carries with it a rejection of responsibility for contraception. Thus these women say:

> Oh, the man should because if you didn't have a man you couldn't get that way.
> I think the husband should. I don't know why, but before I used Norforms. I hated them, I thought they were so messy.

For these women, then, effectiveness depends on their ability to badger their husbands into using condoms; they can be quite punitive on this score since they already have a great deal of suppressed anger because of their husbands' demands.

The ineffective couples in this group often have had as many or more children than they want. The women are generally unhappy about their lack of ability to stop pregnancies, and the husbands often wish also that the problem could be solved, but without trouble to themselves. Their lack of sexual closeness is part of an over-all pattern of disagreement and separateness in marriage. The majority of these couples have been occasional and careless users of contraception. Because they feel they have too many children they have tried to do something to limit them, but they have not been able to co-operate effectively toward this goal. Often they have tried several methods at one time or another; withdrawal, rhythm, condoms, and douching are usually all familiar to them. The woman may have tried a diaphragm but found it "too messy" or "too much trouble."

These women wish that their husbands would take the responsibility for contraception (if they are unwilling to abstain from intercourse, which the women would prefer). At the same time, they sometimes recognize that the men will never do this and seek desperately to find some method both can tolerate. Their underlying attitude toward responsibility is expressed in such statements as these:

> I think the man should [take responsibility] because he knows when he's about to come and I do not. And he's the one who's getting the good out of it, not me.
>
> He doesn't care how many times I get that way; he'd never do anything. The wife [should be responsible] because after the first pleasure the man has no more to do. It's the woman who carries the baby and goes through all the suffering at birth. He goes off to work or gets out of the house and that's all he cares about. He wouldn't use anything at all, he just lets fly. He says that's the only way to get enjoyment; he's selfish enough not to want to miss a second of the pleasure.
>
> I think the husband [should be responsible]; he's the one who causes it, and she will have the trouble, so he ought to think about her.

Their rejection of sexuality and anger about being forced to participate may lead these women to reject contraception itself. They do not effectively separate their very negative feelings about sexual relations from their own self-interest in not having more children. Excess fertility comes to be an ever-present reproach to their husbands. The women feel they have a right to reject the men, but they are not able to act directly to rectify the situation. Their passivity in sexual relations is carried over to family planning; they are not willing to be sufficiently assertive toward their husbands to force effective action.

For their part, the husbands are unwilling to interfere with spontaneous sexual activity and to concern themselves with contraception. As the woman quoted above points out, these husbands often behave as if their actions had nothing to do with pregnancy; that is the woman's problem. Their hostile, eliminative conception of sex means that they get a certain amount of enjoyment from their wives' unhappiness in the relationship, and it also seems likely that their desire to eliminate makes them unwilling to use a condom, since they want to get the semen out of and away from their bodies.

Their wives, on the other hand, do not accept feminine appliance methods. Their rejection of sexuality includes an avoidance of their own genitals; they don't want the mess of any of the feminine appliances. They like the condom for some of the same reasons. It prevents contact with the semen, thus reducing the sexual quality of the relationship as well as preventing pregnancy. This attitude is probably also involved in the fairly common use of the douche for cleanliness after intercourse.

These women's basic attitudes are reflected in some of their more extreme suggestions for limiting the number of children. Two of them jokingly reported these solutions:

> The women with too many children joke about cutting it [the penis] off.
>
> My relatives are always talking about an operation for the man. It's something of a joke for the man to have the operation.

Given the wives' preferences for the condom and their husbands' irritation with it ("He says it's like going swimming with your clothes on"), it is not difficult to understand why these couples have difficulty using a method effectively even though they may half-heartedly experiment with several.

The second type of sexual rejection, the pattern of repressive compromise, occurs in our sample only among effective couples. Here the wife has been successful in repressing her negative feelings about sexual intercourse and manages to maintain that she can "take it or leave it" without either a positive or a negative response. Such an adjustment seems to be accomplished when the husband is willing to be "considerate," which means that he moderates his sexual desires to conform to his wife's wish that intercourse be as infrequent as possible.

The few cases of this type in our sample are all effective at contraception before they have more children than they want. Since the wife is able to persuade the husband to moderate his sexual interests, it is understandable that she is also able to get him to go along with the use of some contraceptive. It is also understandable that these women are themselves willing to take the responsibility for contraception. They have mastered their negative feelings by aggressively seeking enough control of the sexual situation to satisfy the husband's desires without making themselves too unhappy. They are also willing to be energetic about controlling conception and have considerable confidence in their ability to do so, since they think of their husbands as considerate and willing to do what is best. Thus one woman, who uses a jelly alone, told the interviewer:

> The doctor had us use Preceptin because of my health. He didn't think we should have any more children. My husband doesn't mind just as long as it protects me. My health is the most important thing to him. My husband has always been so thoughtful, I never had to worry about it. He always said he was afraid to use condoms because he was afraid they might get a hole in them. The doctor said not to use them, too. He said Preceptin was 99 per cent pure [she probably means effective].

This woman manages to focus the contraceptive issue around her health and in so doing can feel pleased at her husband's considerateness and solicitude. Part of her mastery of sex is in the control of contraception; therefore she is more willing to use feminine appliance methods. Because such women effectively use repression to defend themselves against their negative feelings about sex, they are also able to regard their genitals without the repugnance which many less well-defended working class women feel.

In cases where the husband uses a condom, this kind of woman can find gratification in the idea that he is considerate in this way. Thus one woman spoke of her husband's attitudes in this vein:

> He believes in contraception. He doesn't believe a woman should have too many children too close together. I just think he feels for me. He doesn't think it's good for a woman to have too many children too close. [Who should be responsible?] I think they both should. The wife is more interested as a rule because she's the one that has the babies.

This woman, too, manages to implicate her husband in the aggressive act which she unconsciously feels that sexual relations represent. She has managed to persuade him to be considerate. The less happy women discussed in the section above are not often so lucky; they must contend with men who are much less willing to be "considerate" in the ways they want, and they react with bitterness and resignation to the pregnancies which result. Contraception never becomes for them a subject on which husband and wife can co-operate comfortably. When there is this kind of distance between husband and wife, sex becomes an empty and unpleasant activity to the woman, and pregnancy is the uncalled-for and unjust result. One lower-lower class woman, who has had four children in nine years and who knows very little of contraception, commented about sexual relations in her marriage:

> I guess it's just like everyone else. He just lets me know when he wants to and that's it. Things haven't changed any since we've been married except for having kids. I just take it as part of marriage and don't think any more about it. It don't do nothing for me except give me children. I'd like it less often. I just would. I'm tired most of the time. I'm pregnant now. I don't know of any way it could be better. [How does your husband feel?] It makes him happier and nice around the house. He just thinks that's what a woman is for. It's always his idea to do it.

EXCESS FERTILITY AS AN INTERFERENCE IN SEXUAL RELATIONS

We noted in the previous chapter that slightly less than one-third of the women in our sample indicate a strong ambivalence about their sexuality. These women are not able fully to enjoy intercourse because of interfering anxieties and concerns, although they show some positive disposition toward sexual relations. What bearing, then, does contraceptive behavior have on this kind of ambivalence?

The effective women who fit this pattern show some of the typical concerns one would expect among the working class over being "too sexy" and therefore "bad women." Their concerns are internal, and they generally accept the shortcomings in their sexual relationships as a result of their own feelings. They do not blame their husbands but are rather inclined to speak of them as considerate and understanding about their difficulties. The locus of their ambivalence and the way they think about it will bear examining, for the contrast which it provides with ineffective women's discussions of their difficulties.

Representative of the effective women who have serious interferences with accepting their sexual role is one upper-lower class mother of a three-and-a-half-year-old child. She has been married six years and hopes to have one more child. She told the interviewer:

> I didn't know much before I was married. I read books after I was. My husband was telling me that people do things two or three times a day, and I didn't believe him. I enjoyed being loved, but I was more upset about the embarrassment of undressing together and things like that. I felt that everyone would be staring at me and know what we'd be doing. My two reasons for not cheating, and I'm just joking, are that I got over the embarrassment once and that I might find someone else is better.

> [Now?] I don't get much satisfaction out of it now. I don't know why. My husband and I have discussed it. When he's home on weekends we have it usually. When we lived together [he works out of town now] we made an agreement that we wouldn't have it too often. When you're first married you have it all the time, and after I read the books I decided it was too often. I can take it or leave it. I feel sometimes that I want to, and once we start I change my mind. Sometimes it reassures me that he loves me. I told my husband once that I was in the mood and he has never let me forget it, so I don't do that anymore. Maybe if he was home all the time it would be better. It's more important to him. I think it gives him satisfaction—that's what he says. A woman has to be worked up; a man doesn't need that as much. He tries to be considerate but he usually doesn't get me quite ready. He is always satisfied; I seldom am.

This woman obviously has a strong unconscious belief that to indulge herself sexually would be equivalent to being promiscuous (she "jokes" about cheating) and "bad." Her husband is undoubtedly irritated with her for cutting down the frequency of intercourse, but he also tries to be "considerate" in getting her "ready." We can guess that over the years this couple's relationship will either improve or deteriorate, depending on whether the woman can overcome some of her feelings. In any case, contraception does not pose a great problem in this relationship; husband and wife agree that they should not have more children until their financial situation improves, and the husband is willing to use condoms although he finds them "unpleasant."

Another upper-lower class woman, who has been married for three years and has a two-year-old child, shows a similar pattern, although she feels somewhat more encouraged about gratification in sexual relations:

> Our relations have changed a lot in three years. It was just that we neither one knew much. He wasn't experienced himself, he was only seventeen. I guess it was OK the first year or two. It wasn't *too* good [blushing]. I hardly ever wanted him. He knew it and all men are like that, they can do it anytime and I didn't want to. I thought maybe later on it would change.

> I guess we both know a lot more than we did, and it's better now than before. We know more different ways and positions. We do it about four times a week. He works nights but sometimes when he comes in early in the morning about 9:30 or sometimes about ten in the evening before he goes to work we do it.
>
> Sometimes I care and sometimes I don't. I don't want it most of the time, maybe once a week. The other times it's just for him. I guess I feel I should for his sake. [How is it at best?] Well . . . then I'm satisfied, I guess [smiles]. [And when it is not so good?] I just don't feel *anything*. Sometimes I'm disappointed. When it's not so good I don't want it from the beginning! When I do, it *is*. *He* always finds it satisfying; I can tell by his actions. When I really enjoy it, too, then *he* does more.

This woman seems gradually to have become more at ease in sexual relations; she does not show the same desire to avoid them as the woman quoted above. She was fifteen at marriage and apparently quite ignorant of the facts of life at that time:

> Before I was married I didn't know much. I always thought you had to see a doctor before you got pregnant. My husband never discussed it with me. My mother told me when I was pregnant; I didn't know before that the act led to being pregnant.

In spite of her ignorance and her continuing discomfort about sex, she has been quite assertive about family planning. She knows she does not want more than four children, and she and her husband have agreed to space them. He uses condoms now, but they have obviously discussed and considered other methods:

> He has suggested I use what they call a gold button. My sister had one. The doctor fits that in you and you have to have it taken out and cleaned. . . .
>
> I've heard of a diaphragm. I think it's pretty good. I know it works but it's too much trouble. . . . [Withdrawal?] Oh, we call that "jerking off." We have done that, too, but not *too* much. . . . [Rhythm method?] I've heard of the safe period. I've heard there are three days out of the month you can get pregnant about in the middle of the month. I don't think it would be safe; I think you can get pregnant *any* time.

All the effective women who fit this ambivalent pattern have the feeling that their husbands are considerate and understanding and that they can discuss problems with them. It is apparently not difficult for them to feel some confidence about sexuality; they do not reject sexual relations as meaningless. Also, it is easy for them to feel that contraceptive issues can be worked out co-operatively and without great conflict.

The ineffective women of this type feel quite differently. When a woman is caught between conflicting feelings about sex and also is caught between her own self-interest in not becoming pregnant and her desire to gratify herself and to please her husband, the sexual relationship can become a source of worry and anxiety. At least one-fourth of the ineffective women show this pattern of conflict. A lower-lower class mother, pregnant with her fifth child in nine years of marriage, expressed her problems in this way:

> [What was your knowledge of sex at marriage?] I was too dumb to realize how important it was. It was all fun to me; I had a lot to learn. I thought I was pretty smart, but I wasn't. [Now?] I know when my husband is hot. I'm not a cold one myself, not usually; this pregnancy has been too much. I sure feel rotten all the time nowadays. When we were first married we thought everything was wonderful; we were in love. Sure, I love my husband now, but married love is a lot different than the first kind. We have a bunch of four children now to be responsible for, and there will soon be five. All the things a baby requires! Somehow we manage, but I'm tired of not having enough money most of the time. With a small family you can have a very nice life. I sure love my kids and I wouldn't give them up, but I do think this is the limit.
>
> [How do you feel about sex?] Sure, I feel good, it's natural, but I do not think I need my husband as much as he needs me nor as often. Men usually enjoy marriage more; the man has the best of it. I think if we were not afraid of having children, more than five, we could have a nicer time together and not fight so much. It's only natural; I would have more time for him and want to make him feel good. I think we could have a better life with not too much to fight over. We go to

bed two or three times a week; I'm not sure I would like it less but it is enough.

[What are his feelings?] Sure, he needs it like a starving man needs food. It is important to a man to have a time. I think it is like a tonic to men, makes them feel good. It's nature; that's life. Most women say it is for their husbands. I'm not so sure; I'll bet that plenty of the women have a time themselves but do not make out that it is important to them. I think it is a calmer thing to me, but I like having him love me. Sure, I'm very human. But having babies every year is awful hard on the mother, never gives her a chance to have fun with her kids. She can't take the older ones to the beach or go out with her husband to dance. We are still too young to be tied down like old people. With less kids and more time for the ones we have I'm sure I would be happier and like love and marriage more.

Because there seems no other solution, this woman wants to be sterilized; her husband is sporadic in his use of condoms and she feels she cannot trust the rhythm system. It is clear from her other comments that she and her husband are not able to achieve the restrained and co-operative relationship necessary for effective contraception. The husband's strong desire for intercourse ("like a starving man needs food") may mean that he resists the self-discipline necessary for contraception, and apparently his wife cannot assert herself sufficiently to force him to co-operate. Since she feels isolated, she can only take care of the matter by sterilization if she is going to preserve some sense of satisfaction in her marriage. As she sees it, the situation will shortly become intolerable if she cannot find some way to keep from becoming pregnant. Even so, she is hopeful and does not seek to avoid intercourse.

Other women, who perhaps initially do not so accept their sexual role, seek to master their family limitation problems by reducing the frequency of intercourse. One such wife, also married for nine years and with four children, commented:

Before I was married my girl friends told me a lot of stuff.

> Like your eyes turn in after you have a man. They made me afraid to be with my husband. I was ashamed when we got married. I should have known something before! [Now?] We do it less now and I enjoy it less. He enjoys it more, I do less because I'm afraid every time I'll get a baby for sure. We do it once a week now. It used to be two or three times. I put him away from me now because I'm afraid I'll be pregnant again. I don't enjoy it because I might get stuck with another baby. If I could do it and not get a baby it would be better.

This couple does nothing about contraception; the husband will not accept condoms, and the wife says that douching will not work for her although it may work for other women because "I am stronger [sexually] or something." Like many others in our sample, this woman began marriage with a negative attitude toward sex. She implies that she was able to enjoy intercourse, however, until she became concerned about being pregnant all the time. This concern is so overriding that she can devote little energy to being a "good wife" sexually or to finding gratification in intercourse. Her anxiety about pregnancy reinforces the negative side of her ambivalent feelings about sex; she comes to feel that she cannot afford to have relations and enjoy them, since she has other things to worry about.

This kind of concern undoubtedly affects the husband, too, since he perceives his wife's rejection of him in connection with love-making. Since most working class men do not easily understand their wives' complex feelings about sex, it is easy for them to treat intercourse more and more as their own pleasure. Thus, one lower-lower class mother of five children presented this picture of her situation in the eighth year of marriage:

> I didn't know as much about sex as I thought. Of course, I knew where children came from, but still it's different when you're young and crazy about a fellow. It's different after marriage when there are children to look out for. I knew that what I'd heard about it seemed more fun, like giving myself to him was very important to him. I was disappointed, though; I thought I would like it better. He was better, more loving,

at first. Now it's more relief and that's that. It's about once a week, seldom oftener. He feels that way on weekends or when he isn't working more than when he's tired. Sometimes I feel that way, too, but he isn't here, usually.

One thing I don't like is for him to go to sleep and get rested and then wake me up fooling around. He can get up on time and go to work, but I never get the right sleep and I am cross and have the babies to take care of all day. He knows now that I need my sleep, and if he wants intercourse it has to be early, not in the middle of the night. He lets me know he wants it in different ways, usually he begins pulling at me. Sometimes you can't do much with the kids around. When we were first married he was softer, not rough, not in a hurry because of the girls. He was more careful, too. Sometimes I tell him not to do it, but mostly I get the older kids around and keep them with me until he gets over it or goes out. I want to do it less often.

Sometimes I think I sleep better if I am terribly nervous, but sometimes it is the opposite, it makes me nervous. I knew a woman in the old neighborhood who had to leave her husband because he made her nervous that way. I would like him to be more loving and not so much in a hurry or for him to wait until I wanted it, too. [What are his feelings?] It's nature, men are made that way. He thinks it is the way things should be, and I guess there would not be any children in the world, or not many, if it was otherwise.

Some women pretend they like it more but I know the man has the best of it. They don't have the children, for one thing. He doesn't have any worries about the kids and I do. I can't say it always makes him happy. Most of the time it does, but sometimes he is cross about something else and takes it out on me, not often but he has. He used to say he likes the satisfaction; I think he must get it most of the time. We don't talk that way anymore . . . that was a long time ago.

Here we see that not only pregnancy but also responsibilities to the children already born concerns these women. Both these considerations can be used to bolster negative, avoidant feelings about sexual relations. When the husband is not understanding (when, as in this case, he is unpredictable in his use of condoms), a situation of overt and covert conflict ensues. Excess fertility puts a great deal of pressure on the wife's capacity to handle her responsibilities to her children, her husband, and herself.

The threat of an additional pregnancy provides a further temptation to constrict, to withdraw into simple routines and avoid threatening and energy-consuming intimacies with her husband.

As time goes on in such marriages, the wife becomes more and more dissatisfied and discouraged; her life seems less and less gratifying. She comes to have a sense of inadequacy and deterioration that can be expressed physically as well as psychically:

> It was different from what I thought. I thought I would like it more; I don't mind but it isn't so much fun. I don't see what so many people see in it; love is supposed to make the world go around, but it causes some troubles, too. It hurts my back; my back hurts a long time afterwards and it makes me so lazy that I do not want to work, and it makes my husband lazier than me, he just sleeps and sleeps. I don't mind it two times a week, but if it is more often it runs me down and I have to get up and work with the children to take care of. I don't mind it too much but I do get lazy and feel like resting and not getting up and getting busy. I do not like to be made too tired or weak or lazy.
>
> I think it is the way men are made that they want more and more, and a woman has other things to do and think about. She also has the worry. He is strong; he likes to have his pleasure and then sleep and not think about anything. I find it hard; I get too tired and it hurts my back. It hurts most all day sometimes. I am worried about getting pregnant when I have a job and need to work. There was a time when it was more pleasure for me than now, but that is because I have been sick, and after I am well and healthy I am sure to get pregnant very easy.

It is not difficult to understand that over the years wives with this kind of experience reject sexuality more and more and adopt the attitudes of the women discussed earlier who feel that there is nothing for them in sexual relations but trouble.

In general, then, an examination of the contraceptive attitudes and practices of couples who have differing sexual adjustments suggests the overriding importance of some ability to communicate feelings associated with sex and contraception, to have those views sympathetically considered by both partners, and to act willingly on understandings developed from such communication.

Those couples who share a pattern of genital mutuality usually have also a great deal of intimacy and more general consideration for each other. They find it easy to come to agreement on family planning goals, whether this involves the current use of contraception or its delay. Usually, too, these couples more readily accept feminine appliance methods because they do not have the same deep feelings of anxiety and disgust about manipulating the female genitals. Wives in this group are more likely to accept responsibility for contraception because they feel that the sexual relationship is important to them, also.

One kind of woman who rejects sexuality can nonetheless be effective at contraception. She separates sexual relations from contraception and considers the latter an issue of her own well-being. Such women think of their husbands as considerate and generally manage to make the sexual relationship at least tolerable for them. Because they see contraception as very much in their own interest and because they neutralize their negative feelings about sex, they are better able to accept feminine methods of contraception than are other kinds of ambivalent or rejecting women.

Women who reject sexuality in a more direct and active fashion are inclined to place contraceptive responsibility on their husbands. They are relatively doubtful of feminine methods because of their deep negative attitudes toward their own genitals. They prefer their husbands to use condoms because they wish to avoid contact with the penis and with semen. However, these women often are married to men who take a strongly self-indulgent attitude toward sexual relationships and resist contraceptive interference with their sexual pleasure. Sexual relations become a battleground for these couples, with the wives resisting in a relatively passive way and the husbands demanding their "rights" in a hostile, punitive fashion. This pattern seems most characteristic of the lower-lower class. Excess fertility would be even more a problem to this group were it not that conflicts over sexual relations tend to reduce the frequency of intercourse and therefore make impregnation somewhat less likely.

Difficulties related to family limitation are an added burden on women ambivalent about sexual relations. Where the wife feels her husband to be a considerate, sympathetic person, the couple is often able to adopt an effective method. This is most likely to be the condom, since the woman's underlying feelings about sex make it difficult for her to accept a feminine method. When contraception is effective, the woman feels more hopeful about herself and her marriage and seems to enjoy sexual relations more.

When the couple is unable to co-operate effectively on contraception, such ambivalent women find it increasingly difficult to look forward to sexual relations. Their fear of pregnancy and their sense of fatigue from caring for too many children reinforce their negative feelings about sex. They tend to think of their husbands as unsympathetic to their needs and wishes. They feel that husbands should be responsible for contraception and wish them to use condoms as the only really safe way to prevent the pregnancies they fear. Often, they quite consciously seek to reduce the frequency of intercourse, both to minimize the danger of impregnation and to allow them to build up sexual interest. Their husbands are often self-indulgent in their attitudes and resist using condoms regularly. The wives feel inadequate to insist on the "protection" they want.

The relationship between sexual patterns and contraceptive practices is one of reciprocal influence: mutual enjoyment in sexual relations creates a favorable atmosphere for co-operative family planning and creates minimal interference with carrying it out rationally; difficulties in contraception lead to an increased sense of conflict between husband and wife and to the increasing isolation of both partners—the husband's tendencies toward self-absorbed, hostile expression and the wife's tendencies toward the rejection of sexual love are reinforced. The one exception to this interdependence is the not-too-frequent pattern of repressive compromise, in which the wife succeeds in neutralizing her negative feelings and insists that her husband allow her to be "protected." This, however, requires an uncommon degree of self-assertion on the part of the wife and passive co-operation on the part of the husband.

chapter viii

CONTRACEPTIVE PRACTICE: METHODS AND MEANINGS

This chapter is concerned with the ways in which working class men and women regard particular contraceptive methods in use today, and with the ways they are likely to respond to some methods not now widely used. Most of the discussion in previous chapters has been broader and has not paid particular attention to the actual methods.

Most methods in use today are highly effective compared to non-use, if the couple practices them in appropriate ways. Broadly speaking, in the working class ineffective contraceptive practice has relatively little to do with the technical excellence of the method and much to do with the ways in which people approach the task. However, some methods are more popular in this group than others, and there do seem to be specific relationships between particular methods and particular patterns of marital life. These relationships will be our major concern in the present chapter.

THE MYSTERY OF CONCEPTION

The myth of the birds and the bees has served many generations of parents well. The form may be altered; a scientific phrase replaces the sentimental and the folksy, but the level of understanding is the same. From the beginning of history man has made myths to explain his own beginnings. Some of them may sound quaint or charming now, but they were real and important to the people who believed them. From a belief in ancestral gods reincarnating themselves in the birth of a child to the more "scientific" eighteenth-century belief in the "homunculus," conception has had overtones of the miraculous and elements of mystery. It is difficult to grasp what you cannot see, and for all our society's scientific orientation, conception retains its mystery.

The beliefs evinced by the respondents in our sample range from the animistic to the pseudo-scientific to the scientific. Their views are as vague, concrete, unusual, accurate, rare, and varied as the *Weltanschauungen* of the people themselves. It is also clear that these various beliefs about conception strongly influence attitudes toward family planning and the practice of birth control.

No one in our sample seems not to know that conception comes about as a result of sexual intercourse, although quite a few women indicate that they did not know this (or had repressed the knowledge) at the time they were married. Above this bare minimum, there are several levels of understanding, sometimes coupled with misunderstanding, apparent in our data. A few individuals possess a fairly sophisticated body of knowledge involving an understanding of the role of the ovaries, Fallopian tubes, and uterus, as well as of the fertilization of ovum by sperm. More of our respondents show an understanding only of the latter, and do not differentiate between various parts of the female reproductive system.

Even this level of knowledge is not possessed by the majority of our sample. Some working class men and women do not differentiate between sperm and ovum, and speak instead of more or less identical contributions on the part of men and women which come together to form a "fertile solution." Another group attributes major significance to the man, who is assumed to "lay the egg" in the woman during intercourse; the egg then grows into a baby, sustained by the mother's interuterine nurturance. Finally, a good number of working class men and women do not possess even this level of understanding, and instead can carry their explanation no further than to say that pregnancy results from intercourse by some mechanism they do not know. They may know that intercourse results only if the woman is at her "fertile time," but they do not know how it happens, or they may believe that pregnancy results only if both parties participate fully in the act and have orgasms.

We will discuss these four levels of understanding conception and show how each kind is related to contraceptive practice. First, however, a brief overview of the prevalence of the patterns:

Understanding that Sperm Fertilizes Ovum

More women than men seem aware of this. The men in our sample seem rather disinterested in the mechanisms of conception and regard it as a woman's concern. They are more often content with the bare understanding that without intercourse there is no conception. Among women, in the upper-lower class they more often speak of sperm and ovum; almost half show this level of understanding, compared to about one-fourth of the lower-lower class women.

Undifferentiated Male and Female Contributions

Respondents in this category are most likely to speak of "the man's sperm and the woman's sperm" or of the "stuff" that each partner contributes. About 10 per cent of the whole group speak in these ways.

Since both this and the preceding category involve an

understanding that men and women make contributions to the human being conceived as a result of their intercourse, perhaps there is not an essential difference between the two. In all, almost two-thirds of the upper-lower class women show one of these patterns, compared to about one-third of lower-lower class women. Among men, there are no differences between the two subclasses, about one-third in each class fitting either pattern.

The Father Plants It; the Mother Grows It

This picturesque notion is shared by slightly more than one-fourth of our sample. There seem to be no important class or sex differences in the frequency with which it is held.

Less Knowledgeable Understandings

Only 10 per cent of the upper-lower class women and 40 per cent of the lower-lower class women cannot offer some notion of specific male or female biological contributions. Somewhat more than half the men in both classes content themselves with no explanation beyond this.

While often not very sophisticated, the women in the first two groups understand that two different kinds of substances come together to form the fertilized ovum. Their explanations of how children are conceived run along the following line:

> There is a certain time each month when an egg is dropped, and when the sperm from a man comes in contact with a woman's egg she becomes pregnant. This can only happen once during the month.
> You have to have something to do with your husband; the proper word is a sexual relationship. An egg comes from the

ovary and it is fertilized by the sperm. That's the way I understand it.

You go to bed with your husband. The sperm travels to the egg. The man's sperm determines the sex of the baby. The baby is all hairy when it's inside. It feeds off the afterbirth; even if you don't eat, the baby still feeds off you but it's rough on you.

You get pregnant through intercourse and through your love. You both have to be relaxed and feel a special love for each other that night. I want to get pregnant now and I can't. I think it is because I want to too badly and I do not relax. The sperm meets the egg twelve days before your next period. When you miss a period you know it took. I have a tipped uterus so I have to lie in bed with my feet up after intercourse.

You've got to conceive; the sperm and your discharge have to mix so as to fertilize the egg, and then it goes into the womb and a baby is formed.

It is not clear from what some of these women say where they believe fertilization takes place. Undoubtedly, some of them believe this happens in the vagina. In any case, there is an understanding that sperm and egg have to get together for conception to occur.

Almost no men bother with so detailed an explanation; only women seem enough interested in the matter to learn and remember these facts. This level of knowledge is associated with effective contraceptive practice, and particularly with the use of a feminine appliance method. Of the sixteen women in our sample who share this view, seven now use a feminine appliance method (diaphragm, suppositories, vaginal jelly alone, or tablet), one has used such a method previously, and four expect to change from their present practice to the diaphragm. In all, then, three-fourths of the women who have this view are receptive to a feminine method. Of the women who use such a method, seven out of ten hold this view. In contrast, the women who do not use a feminine method and are not interested in one tend to be considerably less knowledgeable in their understanding.

It thus appears that feminine appliance methods require some more sophisticated understanding of the mechanics of conception than just the idea that intercourse causes pregnancy or that the man "lays the egg." Because of their more complex understanding, women of this type are able to appreciate more fully how a feminine method works and are less likely to feel that if the semen enters the vagina all is lost.

As noted, the group who speak of equivalent male and female contributions (each contributes an "egg" or "sperm") is small, only about 10 per cent. There are no notable differences in the methods used by those who speak in this way. Perhaps it is just that they have not paid sufficient attention to terminology to name the two components separately, because in other respects their understanding is more or less equivalent to that of the group discussed first. Typical of this version of conception are these comments:

> Everybody knows what causes pregnancy. The male sperm makes contact with the female sperm. There are hundreds of them, I guess, and you go through an ovation [sic] period.
> The husband's cells get caught with the mother's cells in intercourse and they get together and get a baby. I understand what happens but it's hard to say it.
> I understand it's during your fertile time. The mother's egg and the father's get together. I always watch it. The woman's inside is open seven days before and seven days after your period.
> There are only three days a month a woman can get pregnant so the two germs have to connect. Then a child is formed. This is really all I know.

In all, 80 per cent of the women who use feminine appliance methods effectively have one of these two views of conception, compared to 38 per cent of the women who are effective with other methods, and one-third of the ineffective women.

The view that "the man lays the egg" is held by about a quarter of the men and women in our sample. It is a view favored by about twice as many men as women. The ideas involved are expressed in this way:

> My understanding is that the man lays an egg in you. Sometimes the egg is fertile, sometimes it isn't. If it is you're pregnant.
>
> There is a sperm that leaves the man's body and enters the organs of the woman's body and when it reaches there it either takes life or not if it's during the time when she can conceive.
>
> I guess he has what you call a seed and it goes into the woman and it goes up and it grows until it becomes a baby.
>
> The sperm travels through the male, and if she is ready she will catch the sperm and it will grow more and more every day.
>
> The man puts his thing into the woman's kitty cat, that's what Joe calls woman's privates. I just found out from the doctor about the stuff that goes into the woman. He told me about all that stuff, but I was too ashamed to listen.

Where attention is focused on the man's "stuff," the contraceptive that seems most sensible is the condom, since this is the technique that most effectively prevents the man's "germ" or "egg" from taking root in the womb. When the woman also understands something about the "fertile time," the rhythm method also makes sense since at other times the man's egg cannot start growing. Neither of the two women in this category who use feminine appliance methods does so out of free choice; one uses Preceptin at her doctor's insistence, and the other uses a diaphragm because her husband refuses to use condoms. For most women of this type, it is condoms or rhythm or nothing. Since most of them have had unhappy experiences with the rhythm method, condoms seem the only sensible method. Among the ineffective couples, when the husband resists condoms the woman feels there is no other way to prevent his "laying the egg" except to reduce the frequency of intercourse.

The less knowledgeable men and women just do not want to think about conception and how it comes about. For them, the event is simply a natural consequence of intercourse, and no further information is necessary or desirable. The defensiveness with which men sometimes respond suggests that the subject is so mysterious to them that they would prefer not to try to understand it. They often avoid the question with such responses as:

Now, we both know the answer to that. When you have intercourse the wife can become pregnant, that's all.

Women are more likely to admit that they do not know what happens:

> I call it nature and it can't be helped. You just accept it and go on. I can't explain it.

If pressed, these people would probably admit that the man's ejaculation has something to do with conception. They presumably have ideas not too different from those of the group discussed above, who explain no further than to ascribe central importance to the semen. In both cases, the condom method makes most sense because it is the only one that effectively isolates the penis and its secretions from the woman's body. None of the women who use feminine contraceptive devices fall into this minimum-knowledge category. The three effective condom users who claim no detailed knowledge about conception are all women who reject sexuality; it is not surprising that they also do not want to learn about a subject so closely connected with intercourse. Since their husbands will use condoms consistently, they have no reason to learn more about conception.

In summary, then, inadequate and male-dominated notions about the mechanics of conception tend to encourage use of the condom and, to a lesser extent, of rhythm. By and large, only those respondents who have some understanding of fertilization of ovum by sperm are receptive to feminine appliance methods, since an appreciation of such methods requires an understanding of this aspect of conception.

METHODS OF CONTRACEPTION

The methods of contraception in general use in the United States today are the condom, the diaphragm, the rhythm system, and the douche. About three-fourths of our working class sample was using one or another of these methods at least occasionally at the time of our interview. Vaginal suppositories, not widely used in the general population, are currently being used by four of our respondents. Withdrawal, vaginal tablet, and vaginal jelly netted one user each, bringing the total group to over 85 per cent. Two-thirds of the ineffective group were using some contraceptive occasionally—half were using a douche and most of the others a condom.

About half the respondents had experience with more than one contraceptive method. Only 40 per cent of the effective respondents were still using the first method they had tried. About 40 per cent of the ineffective users had tried more than one method; about one-fourth had not experimented with any; and about one-third had tried only one method.

A good many respondents, then, know of more than one contraceptive method from personal experience, and most know of others from conversations with close friends, co-workers, and relatives. This first- and second-hand knowledge leads them to have more or less well formulated ideas about the widely used methods—more than one might expect, given the normal reticences assumed to apply to so private a matter. We will discuss below their dominant ideas about the major methods as they are expressed by users and non-users.

The Condom

This is the most widely used and widely known method in the United States (Freedman, Whelpton, and Campbell, 1959). It is known to almost all our respondents; nearly half the effective couples use condoms and almost as many of the ineffective ones either use condoms now or have tried them in the past. Several assets and drawbacks appear when respondents discuss the condom, and the meanings implicit in their ideas are important in the choice or rejection of this method.

Among the good things about the condom, respondents mention the following characteristics:

It is used by the man. This is, perhaps, the most central aspect of the condom's meaning. For the many women who do not wish to become involved with sex too intimately, who want their participation to be as passive as possible, the fact that the man wears the condom makes it especially attractive. Contraception at the most concrete technical level becomes his responsibility and worry. If the wife can trust her husband, she does not have to be at all active in contraception. Women who reject sexuality or who are ambivalent about it generally prefer that the man "take care of things" in this way.

It is a visible, external device. There can be no doubt when the condom is properly in place, and it cannot get lost. When it is where it belongs, it is clearly there. Thus, it appeals as the least complex device. The condom is worn in a familiar way, as the many associations to "clothes," "shoes," or "gloves" suggest.

It fits with simple, male-dominated ideas about conception. Because of the mechanical barrier between the man's sexual products and the woman, the condom seems most directly to deal with many working class people's ideas about conception. If they believe that the man "lays the egg" or that a fertile solution is formed when his ejaculation comes into contact with the woman's "insides," clearly the most sensible course is to prevent the semen from reaching the woman's internal genitalia. Respondents can feel great security so long as they know that what the man has ejaculated is thrown away with the condom.

It effectively separates the genitals and their products. Given many women's negative attitudes about sex, concretely expressed in their desire to avoid contact with semen, the condom can be attractive on non-contraceptive grounds as well. Those women who reject sexuality or who wish to minimize its emotional impact can feel better because they know that sexual contact has been attenuated by the thin film of latex. This idea was reflected most directly by one woman who explained her dislike of feminine appliance methods and her preference for the condom by saying, "I don't like to have what I call his 'load' in me."

The characteristics that are assets in the eyes of some respondents can also mean liabilities for others; the other side of the coin can produce strong resistance to the method in spite of the advantages seen in it.

It interferes with the man's pleasure. This is a belief among men and one which they readily communicate to their wives. Many ineffective couples are ineffective because the man resists the regular use of condoms and his wife will tolerate no other method. Wives who accept sexuality more readily are likely to sympathize with their husbands' dissatisfaction and seek out some other method, although often they must first overcome negative feelings about feminine methods. It is possible that the man's dislike of condoms—"like taking a bath with your shoes on"—is based as much on the psychological meaning of lack of contact as on diminished physical sensation. Men who have eliminative ideas about intercourse are particularly inclined to resist this interference with full, ejaculatory elimination of the seminal products. More often than not, such men are married to women who specifically want to prevent this elimination.

It might break. This is a very common anxiety, even with couples who use the condom. Most often, however, it is more an excuse for its non-use or sporadic use than a real concern. Ineffective women, particularly, are inclined to excuse their careless pattern of contraceptive behavior by suggesting that the condom may break, anyway. Even for effective couples, the idea that the condom might break or develop a small hole is a hedge against taking responsibility for an "accident."

The woman is at the man's mercy. A small minority of women dislike the condom because they must trust their husbands to use it. As several of our respondents know from experience, a husband who is not "considerate" and "careful" may fail to use a condom without telling his wife. A few women decide that they will be better off if they take matters into their own hands and adopt some feminine method. For most working class women, however, this is simply an inevitable disadvantage against which the only recourse is some degree of insistence that the husband take proper care.

Underlying the various assets and disadvantages is a common core of symbolic meaning for this method. At the broadest level, the condom represents some denial of sexuality in its full marital context. It is known first as the method of the single man anxious to avoid disease or the proverbial shotgun. Some of the men in our sample told the interviewer quite proudly that they had not used condoms since becoming married; for them the method accompanied illicit relations. It is perhaps the most "unnatural" of the appliance methods of contraception, in spite of being the simplest, because of the mechanical barrier it interposes between the genitals. When a couple is sufficiently concerned about family limitation and unable to accept another method, they may be willing to use the condom. Resistance to its unnaturalness, however, makes backsliding easy for many of them, particularly for the men. Typically, men who use condoms reflect a kind of resignation about the method ("I don't mind them, I guess"); seldom are they enthusiastic about what they do.

The Diaphragm

The diaphragm is primarily a middle class contraceptive; only a small proportion of working class women have adopted it. According to Freedman, Whelpton, and

Campbell (1959), the diaphragm is used three times as often by college graduate women as by women who have attended only grammar school. In our sample, the diaphragm was currently used by slightly over 10 per cent of the respondents, and an equal proportion had previously tried the method and given it up. Because it is not as simply and easily comprehended as the condom, reactions to the diaphragm are not so clearly organized. Most women and quite a few men in our sample had heard of the method, but their understanding of it varied a great deal.

Aside from the respondents who now use the diaphragm, few men and women in our sample could see assets in it. The values attributed to it by users are mainly these:

The wife can feel secure because she's in control. Women who use the diaphragm feel greater mastery of the situation because they themselves use the contraceptive device. When the husband has been restive about condoms, the wife feels less uneasy that contraception will be omitted because of his self-indulgence. These women, of course, believe the diaphragm to be highly effective, and often their confidence is increased because the appliance has been prescribed by a physician and not just purchased in a drugstore.

The husband's pleasure is not spoiled. The diaphragm allows the couple to avoid some of the condom's drawbacks. For those couples who enjoy a mutual sexual relationship, it can be quite attractive:

> We feel it is the best and most pleasant. We tried rubbers but John didn't like it. I heard about this thing and went to a doctor to be fitted for it. I feel it is the best protection and we are both happier with the satisfaction we get.
>
> The diaphragm is very good. The woman inserts it in her womb. The man doesn't feel it at all.

For women who enjoy sexual relations, the fact that the husband enjoys intercourse more with a diaphragm than with the condom increases their own pleasure and makes them feel like better wives.

Those who do not use the diaphragm are vociferous in their uncertainties or criticisms; apparently the idea of a method which requires the woman to insert a solid object into her vagina arouses a good deal of anxiety.

The diaphragm is mysterious in its workings. Many working class men and women have heard just about enough about the diaphragm to feel that it is a strange appliance. Because they do not understand much about the woman's internal genitalia, it is difficult for them to imagine how the diaphragm might work. While the condom's effectiveness is obvious, since it prevents the entrance of the seminal fluid into the woman's body, the diaphragm has no such manifest function—unless one has clearly in mind that fertilization takes place in another part of the reproductive system. Many working class people try to think of the diaphragm as a "woman's rubber" but this analogy does not get them very far since a little knowledge of the appliance makes them realize that it does not preserve a total separation between the penis and the vagina.

How do you know when it's working? Because the diaphragm is out of sight, it is difficult for many respondents to feel any confidence in it. Women worry that they might make a mistake in inserting it or that it will become dislodged during intercourse.

> I wouldn't like it. I wouldn't like the idea of putting it in and taking it out. You can't see it and you would never know whether it was in right or not. This way you can't go wrong with the rubber; there's only one way to put it on.
>
> I just don't trust them. They're not safe. All a woman has to do is turn them and they're not safe.

It's messy and too much trouble. The use of jelly and the fact that the woman must make contact with her genitals in inserting and withdrawing the diaphragm signifies to many women that this method will be messy and unpleasant. Such women avoid their genitals as much as possible, particularly in connection with sexual relations. Furthermore, the method seems troublesome to them; it requires a more prolonged interruption of sexual activity than does the condom, since almost no women are willing routinely to insert the diaphragm before going to bed. Thus, respondents commented:

> The diaphragm is too much trouble. A woman doesn't know when it's going to happen and I never let my wife know in advance.
> When you use a diaphragm . . . well, you never know when you're going to have sexual relations. It may happen in the middle of the night and you have to go fiddle around with the diaphragm, and you get back to bed and your husband may be asleep.
> I'm sure it's safe if you insert it right but it sounds like a lot of trouble.

It requires that the woman initiate contraception. A good many women, and some men, do not like the idea that the woman should take responsibility for contraception in this way. Women who reject sexuality feel that they should not have to be the ones to make the contraceptive effort: "Why should I have to worry with it; if he wants it, let him put something on himself." Perhaps one reason why women who reject the idea of a diaphragm more readily accept "the gold button," as they call it, is that with this method the physician takes the responsibility for inserting and taking out the appliance. Thus, the same woman who says the husband should "put something on" speaks approvingly of a friend who got a "button."

> There's another way. A girl friend of mine had five kids and she got pregnant again and she went for an abortion, and this doctor put a button in her and she doesn't ever take it out. She has to go to him about every year and he changes it.

Men sometimes have an underlying reluctance to permit their wives to take over a function so closely related to intercourse. Thus one man makes the symbolic equation between feminine initiative and the bad woman in this way:

> I've heard of diaphragms. I've seen them. I've known people what used them. But I wouldn't want that in my wife. It's not right. It's like prostitutes, doing it for business.

When a wife has more children than she wants, she may feel justified in assuming the initiative by using some feminine method; before that time, many working class men and women feel that it is somehow unseemly for the woman to do so.

It provokes fear of physical loss or damage. Many of our respondents are afraid that damage may result from using a diaphragm. Their two major concerns are that it will be lost inside the woman's body, and that it will damage her internally. Many of these people's ideas about female internal genitalia make this seem quite possible, although if one were to pin them down in rational discussion they probably would not be able to say exactly where they think the diaphragm would go when "lost." Closely related to this concern is a fear that the diaphragm might become stuck, so that it could not be withdrawn without a doctor's help. We know from other studies that many working class women have similar fears about tampons.

The fear that the woman can hurt herself with the diaphragm is similarly widespread. Respondents express these fears along the following lines:

> It keeps you safe but it hurts very much. None of my friends use it.
>
> I'd be afraid to let my wife use it; wouldn't it hurt her?

Just as a fear of the diaphragm's getting lost is irrational and not clearly formulated, fears that the woman might hurt herself are poorly thought out. Often these concerns pose a strong barrier to the use of a diaphragm, even when it is prescribed, because it is difficult for these women to examine their concerns rationally and to find reassuring answers. Thus, one woman gave up on the diaphragm after a year's use because she could never feel comfortable with it or with herself in charge of contraception:

> I tried the diaphragm. I stopped using it because it hurt me. It just bothered me. I couldn't insert it, my husband had to. It was more trouble to my husband than it was for him to use something himself. I would say the diaphragm is effective, but as far as I am concerned, I just can't use it. I do believe in it. I felt it was more effective than having my husband using something.

The diaphragm is clearly regarded as a potent device in the sense that it is brought into close contact with the delicate female genitals and has the capacity both to hurt them and to prevent conception. Its potency is further enhanced by the fact that only physicians may prescribe it, unlike other methods that may be freely purchased at the drugstore. Furthermore, it is a more "mature" contraceptive than the condom, and fits with marriage rather than with bachelorhood. It assumes a more sophisticated knowledge of the user's anatomy and more acceptance of herself as a sexual being. For both these reasons, the diaphragm seems most appropriate to middle class people, who are assumed to be more rational and more at home with its "medical" connotations. Working class women shy away from such authoritative and scientific things; even after having had several children, a woman may be unable to discuss contraception with her physician and may become so embarrassed if he broaches the subject himself that she does not understand what he tells her.

Suppositories

Less than one-fifth of our effective users now employ suppositories, and still fewer had used them and changed to another method. However, a few points about this technique are of general interest for what they suggest about the possibilities of other feminine contraceptive methods.

The suppository is analogous to the condom in certain ways. It is a feminine method which, like the condom, is readly procurable and which requires no particular skill or training. Respondents can use it without feeling that they need medical advice. Knowledge about the suppository is spread by word-of-mouth within the group, and an awareness of the various brands is encouraged by advertising (which, to be sure, does not mention its contraceptive nature). The suppository is attractive to women exactly because it is relatively accessible through normal consumer channels; it does not seem as "special" as the diaphragm, for example, or even vaginal jellies. It can be treated in the same matter-of-fact way as other drugstore purchases—toothpaste, aspirin, or sanitary napkins.

The women who have used suppositories but do not like them complain that they are messy, but their comments do not have the same emotional loading as similar comments about the diaphragm and jelly method, presumably because the required contact with the genitals is not as elaborate. It appears that the relatively solid form of the suppository decreases feelings about messiness. On the other hand, the fact that the suppository melts as the diaphragm does not, means that fear of damage to the genitals does not arise so readily. When one considers that in our sample as many women employ suppositories (with no authoritative medical support) as employ the diaphragm (prescribed by their physicians), it is apparent that simpler feminine techniques such as this would have considerable possibilities were they promoted more forcefully.

The Rhythm System

This non-appliance method of contraception has many features attractive to working class men and women. However, the complexity of the calculations involved and the uncertainties about exactly how they are made make it difficult for most people to entertain rhythm seriously. Historically, the method has been the subject of elaborate "numbers games" with a variety of rules offered for calculating the "safe period" (Lewinsohn, 1956). Most of our respondents are aware that abstinence at some time during the menstrual cycle may have a contraceptive effect. However, few have any clear-cut understanding of how the method might be effectively pursued; most assume that one must abstain at some time during the middle of the period, but they are vague about how this is reliably to be done. Almost none of our respondents mention the use of a thermometer and charting in connection with rhythm. Instead, they content themselves with rules of thumb; one woman considers herself "safe" after the first eleven days of her menstrual period; another says she is safe except between the twelfth and sixteenth days; and one man reported that he had intercourse with his wife only three days before and three days after her period.

From another study (Freedman, Whelpton, and Campbell, 1959) we know that rhythm is much more widely practiced among couples of higher status, principally Catholics. According to that study, only 16 per cent of grammar-school-educated Catholic women had used this method, compared to 42 per cent of college graduates. Even so, a fair number of women in our sample say they have tried the method and given up after becoming pregnant. Many women, both Protestant and Catholic, tell us that they cannot use rhythm because their periods are irregular or because they are "overfertile" and can become pregnant at any time. Their general attitude is that rhythm would be nice if it worked, but "it doesn't work for me."

It should be clear from what has been said about working class people's abilities and capacities for planning that rhythm practiced in an effective way is not a real possibility. Temperatures must be charted, or some very systematic counting system that allows wide latitude for the fertile period must be used. The complexity of this "natural system" makes understandable the fact that college women use it most frequently, for they have both the trained skills and the discipline to do so.

Given the general distrust of this method, it seems unlikely that working class women seriously interested in contraception will use it. Those less strongly motivated may play at the rhythm system, but they do so more as a fairly easy way of helping chance than with any real sense of conviction.

Withdrawal

Like rhythm, withdrawal seems widely known as a method, and widely distrusted. Only one person in our sample reported the consistent use of the method, and this was a woman who has been married for twenty-four years. Others reported trying the method from time to time, usually early in marriage when they were not too concerned about pregnancy, and certainly not in any consistent and disciplined manner.

Withdrawal is thought to be both unsafe and unfair to the husband. Few wives are so trusting of their husbands that they believe the method could be used more than once in a while without failure through the man's refusal to withdraw. Most of the men interviewed were quite emphatic in their rejection of it: those who are effective in contraception regard their present method as more satisfying; those who are not seem to feel that it is too much to ask of a man.

Women's attitudes vary according to their feelings about their husbands' enjoyment of sexual relations. Those who accept sexuality feel that withdrawal would be at least unfair, if not unhealthy, for the man. Those who reject sexuality often say that they think withdrawal would be a good method if their husbands could be trusted to withdraw in plenty of time. Since their husbands seldom share this view, however, they do not think seriously of using the method. For most couples, then, the shortcomings of other methods are not such that withdrawal represents an attractive alternative.

The Douche

Before World War II, douching was apparently the most widely used contraceptive method in this country (Riley and White, 1940). Today, according to Freedman, Whelpton, and Campbell (1959), about one-fourth as many couples use this method. The decline is accounted for by the increasing popularity of the condom, the diaphragm, and rhythm. However, it is still more widely used among lower class people than among those of higher class status, probably because of the greater tolerance lower class people have for ineffective methods.

Among our respondents, douching shares the position of rhythm: many say that it is good but unsafe. Because a fair number of these women believe in douching for cleanliness, the idea of douching for contraception also is attractive. As with rhythm, many have tried it, usually with vinegar, but have given up because it has not worked. Most of the douche users are relatively sporadic; they tell us that "sometimes I wash myself out." Because they have relatively little faith in the method anyway and because they feel that contraception is not something over which they have real control, this gesture in the direction of effectiveness is more symbolic than earnest. For most of our respondents, then, both rhythm and douching are rather half-hearted efforts at contraception tried as the couple moves from non-use to effective use of limitation techniques. If family limitation is pursued vigorously, they usually shift to another method after a failure or two.

New Contraceptive Methods

Respondents were asked about three relatively new methods: vaginal jellies designed for use without a diaphragm (marketed for several years but not widely used), the vaginal tablet (one brand of which is marketed in some parts of the country), and the oral pill (now available only on a prescription basis). We will briefly assess here the response that working class men and women made to these methods, but the reader must bear in mind that their reactions were on the basis of very sketchy descriptions and provide only a rough guide to the ways these methods might be received if more fully presented to the group by physicians or clinics.

Only one woman in the sample used a vaginal jelly. A fair number of respondents had heard of it, but most had not. The method is considered to have something in common with the diaphragm and jelly method, but is simpler and is thought to be less effective. As with the diaphragm, some clear understanding of conception is required to understand how such a method can work. Because the technique cannot be checked by sight, there is much uncertainty about its use, and working class people would need strong reassurance by physicians if they were to have any sense of conviction about its effectiveness.

Aside from the issue of effectiveness (and any new technique is certain to meet with disbelief without strong medical authority communicated to the individual in a direct and fairly simple way), the major objection to this method has to do with its "messiness." Women tell us, "I'd never put all that stuff inside me; it would be too messy." This seems to be the standard response to any method that requires the woman to put something into her vagina. At the same time, it is clear to women that this method would be simpler and would require less manipulation than the diaphragm and jelly, and it is appealing on that score.

The central difficulty in understanding this method, or the one that follows, is the lack of any clear idea of the spermicidal action of jellies, creams, or tablets. Part of these people's suspiciousness is that they do not understand how these substances prevent conception. If they were able to understand that such methods prevent fertilization by "neutralizing" the sperm and that this is done in a predictable way, their acceptance would increase.

Almost none of the respondents had ever heard of the vaginal tablet. When the interviewer explained to them that a tablet inserted into the vagina would prevent conception, the response was often one of suspicion. It is difficult for many working class men and women to understand how this might work. Women are not sure that such a method could be "safe," i.e., effective. Because they have no clear idea of how a spermicidal contraceptive operates, it is difficult for them to imagine a successful technique that does not pose a mechanical barrier between sperm and ovum.

On the other hand, quite a few respondents thought that if a tablet were really effective, it would be a very attractive method. None of the women complained that it might be messy; apparently the fact that the tablet is solid reduces such concerns. While this method still requires women to touch their genitals, there is not the added source of unpleasantness stemming from the "messy" product itself. If the tablet dissolves, the liquid that results is assumed not to be greasy, as the jellies are, but more or less unnoticeable.

In general, both these methods probably have greater possibilities in the working class than their current use would indicate. If these people's initial disbelief in techniques that seem so simple can be overcome, it is likely that working class women would use such methods more consistently than the diaphragm and jelly. We have seen that many women feel blocked in their efforts at effective contraception because their husbands will not use condoms regularly and they know of no feminine method that does not seem intimidating or ineffective. Given an opportunity to learn of these two simpler methods, some of these women might be able to achieve effective contraception.

The idea of an oral pill is very attractive. Most respondents say that a pill that was easy to take would be the perfect answer to contraceptive problems because it would be clean, because it could be taken before sexual activity began, and because the woman would feel secure all the time. None of the respondents felt that it would be too much trouble to take a pill every day, although a few worried that so many pills would be expensive.

There is some feeling, however, that a pill that would really work would be too potent. Thus, men and women commented along the following lines:

> I would never take pills for something like that. What if they did not really work and a baby was coming and you did not know it yet? Couldn't pills deform the baby, maybe make it a cripple?
>
> I don't think I'd want to do it because if they are strong enough to keep you from getting pregnant they must do other damage. If they're that strong it might affect your sexual organs if it's strong enough to keep you from getting pregnant.
>
> That's no good. I wouldn't let my wife take it. I think anything going into the bloodstream would be an injury.

The idea of an oral pill potent enough to prevent pregnancy thus arouses anxieties about being desexed, sterilized, poisoned, or damaged in some other way. (It is interesting that men reject a pill for themselves much more violently than they do one for women, and their wives tend to agree that a woman's pill would not be as dangerous or desexing as a man's). We know that lower class people are generally suspicious of medicine; they tend to visit physicians only when they must, and they avoid taking drugs (apart from simple remedies) because of the kind of fears suggested above. When a medicine seems designed to affect sexual functioning, these feelings come even more strongly to the fore.

In spite of these objections, the attraction of a simple oral method would undoubtedly result in its use by working class women if they were given encouragement and reassurance against its being in some way "poisonous." A basic problem with this method, however, is the difficulty created by having to take a pill every day. Given the personalities of many lower-lower class women and the difficulties they have in consistently planning and following routines that do not seem "natural," it is unlikely that many of them would be successful in following the regimen necessary if the method is to be effective. A "pill a day" system provides too many opportunities for forgetfulness or carelessness for many of these women to be regarded with much confidence. While clinics that provide their patients with support and encouragement in using such a technique may succeed in imbuing them with a sense of regularity, it seems likely that when the pill is sold more casually and routinely, working class women will backslide fairly quickly.

On the other hand, were a pill developed that needed to be taken only once a month (for example, during or at the end of the menstrual period), the chances for successful adoption in this group would be much greater. In short, the idea of an oral contraceptive is enormously appealing. If a method is developed that does not require rigorous once-a-day scheduling, it is likely to be adopted widely after the initial anxiety about being "drugged" has worn off.

chapter ix

℞ FOR FAMILY PLANNING IN THE WORKING CLASS

IN THE PREVIOUS CHAPTERS we have described the social and psychological character of working class life and individuals that strongly influence these people's ability to formulate family planning goals and pursue them effectively by the use of contraceptive methods. Here we will discuss some of the implications of our findings for various kinds of family planning and contraceptive programs as they may be carried out in connection with hospital clinics, private medical practice, Planned Parenthood clinics, social case work, and general public education. Undoubtedly, practitioners in this field will see other implications as they match their own professional experience against the study's findings.

It is clear from this examination of attitudes, behaviors, and motives that those who wish to encourage the working class, and particularly its lower portion, to practice contraception consistently and effectively have a difficult problem. It is a problem with no quick or easy solutions either in technical innovations or in educational and clinical programs. The lack of effective contraception so common in this group is not due simply to ignorance or misunderstanding; *it is embodied in particular personalities, world views, and ways of life which have consistency and stability and which do not readily admit such foreign elements as conscious planning and emotion-laden contraceptive practices.*

On the other hand, it is also clear that there is a solid motivational base to encourage many working class husbands and wives to have fewer children than they are likely to have. If some simple, magical solution were available, a great many would take advantage of it. Since such a solution will probably not become available, the practical worker in the field is confronted with the problem of working from a weak motivational base in favor of contraception and helping his clients to thread their way through the various social and psychic interferences.

EDUCATIONAL EFFORTS

In this category we place the variety of efforts that might be made through direct and mass media techniques to inform and persuade about contraception.

It is clear from our data (and somewhat surprising to us) that many of our respondents, both effective and ineffective users of contraceptives, have read something about sex and contraception. This suggests that there is a "market" and an "audience" for such materials if they are properly and interestingly presented. Further, it is also clear that our respondents are not really lacking in minimal information about contraception; most know of at least two methods that would be effective if they were practiced. We suggest that the problem here is not one of simple knowledge but of making knowledge meaningful to the people themselves.

One reason why it is difficult for many working class couples to make their knowledge meaningful is that they know so little about their own and their spouse's genitals and about conception. It is difficult for them to have any sense of conviction about methods other than the condom since they cannot see what difference the method makes and they have little understanding to substitute for seeing and feeling. Educational efforts that enable these people to link up the method itself with more understanding of what it accomplishes would perhaps make it easier for them to adopt effective contraception.

Many working class people, particularly women, would probably be interested in a book that explains these matters in simple and meaningful fashion. A book will probably carry more authority than a comic magazine, even though it may not reach as many readers. Perhaps a program can be initiated whereby such material is mailed to prospects. Two groups relatively easy to reach occur to us—newly-weds (whose names can be secured from marriage license registers) and recent mothers (whose names can be secured from birth registrations). In the case of newly-weds in particular, a book (or booklet) also including information on sexual relations would be useful. The content of such a book, however, would need to be less impersonal and detached than many now in use—perhaps the approach of the better "family problem" columnists would be useful.

In the general education area, too, slow progress is made by articles in the mass media, particularly those which specifically reach the working class. Over a period of time, such articles can do much to change attitudes. Perhaps their most valuable function is to prepare the ground for contacts with clinics and personal physicians, to create readiness for contraceptive instruction. One negative point should be made, however. Many such articles are confusing to working class readers because of their general ignorance in this area. Particularly when an article becomes a brief encyclopedia of methods is the reader likely to be left up in the air. He does not know which method to choose and therefore finds it easy to continue what he does (or does not) do.

Finally, advertising is a further source of education which, so far as we know, is unused today. If the companies in this field could do so without arousing damaging opposition, much could be accomplished by well-conceived advertising campaigns. This is, after all, how most Americans learn about technical innovations. It is particularly the way in which the working class, isolated from the mainstream of our society, learns to regard as desirable many activities that require accessory products (brushing teeth and bathing, for example). We are aware that there may be reasons other than public opposition for restricting publicity on contraceptives, but we suggest that if working class ineffectiveness is considered a really serious problem, advertising policies merit serious re-examination.

METHODS

We have indicated some of the implications of working class attitudes toward particular contraceptive methods in the previous chapter. Here we will note in summary form some of the more important ones.

The *condom* will probably be the method chosen by most working class couples for a long time. It fits too well with many of their ideas about conception, sexual relations, and the genitals to be easily discarded in favor of technically or esthetically superior feminine appliances. Physicians and clinics might consider being more liberal in prescribing condoms for couples who seem to have sufficient motivation to use them.

The *diaphragm-and-jelly* method carries many disadvantages from the point of view of working class couples. It can never be expected to become widespread among this group so long as their attitudes on this general subject do not change drastically.

The simpler *vaginal jellies* or *tablets* have more promise for this group. Although they require the woman to come into some contact with her genitals, the contact is less extensive than with the diaphragm. Adequate persuasive efforts could perhaps result in much wider adoption of these methods. The vaginal tablet may be adopted more easily than the jellies. It is a solid which stays in that state until the tablet is in the vagina, so that notions of messiness are diminished. The one drawback is the ease with which these women may convince themselves that the method is too simple to be effective. Careful attention will have to be paid to explaining that it does work and to giving some simple, convincing rationale for its success.

We are aware that there is considerable medical reluctance to foster simpler methods that do not seem as effective as the more complex or demanding ones. This makes good sense for the practitioner who deals with middle class patients from whom he can expect control and rationality. From the social scientist's point of view, it makes very little sense for a working class couple which is doing nothing, or doing something only sporadically. A method that 50 per cent of the couples acquainted with it will use but that is only 85 per cent effective is certainly superior to one that only 15 per cent of the couples will use even though it be 95 per cent effective.

From the responses of men and women in our sample, we doubt that the *oral contraceptive* now being publicized will prove widely successful among this group. At a more superficial level, there will be a number of women who will fear its possibly "poisonous" effects, just as many working class people are reluctant to take potent drugs and will do so voluntarily only when they feel desperately ill. More basic than this is the difficulty raised by having to take a pill every day. These people find it difficult to plan consistently or to follow routines that do not seem "natural." It is unlikely that many women in the working class (other than those with more than four children who become desperate about pregnancies) will follow a strict daily pill-taking regimen.

A pill to be taken once a month, or even once a week, would present an entirely different picture. The more basic difficulties listed above would no longer apply, and there would be only the problem of overcoming more general fears of drugs. The possibility of taking contraceptive action separated from the sexual act and from interaction with the husband would make such a pill very attractive to this group.

IN-CLINIC PRACTICE

Since we have no systematic information about clinical practice, we can make only a few general comments. We see the greatest problem as that of getting women to come to the clinic or to their physician. However, we have enough respondents who, for example, have had an opportunity to discuss contraception with a physician and to get a diaphragm, either in a clinic or from a private physician, to know that women often find these professional contacts not convincing or enlightening enough to overcome resistance on their own or their husbands' part.

What is a simple matter of contraception to the doctor or nurse is a much more complex emotional issue to the patient. Often the patient finds that she leaves the professional without having become enough involved to retain what she presumably learned, either about the method itself or about the reasons for it. Some effort needs to be made to communicate more fully with these women in their contacts with professionals—both to teach them more about conception and contraception as it applies to them as individuals and to help them view their genitals more neutrally so that they can be matter-of-fact about using feminine contraceptives. (Gynecologists in private practice who fail to have the patient insert the diaphragm while in the office, for example, place a heavy burden on their patients' maturity and self-control, a burden which many cannot easily assume.)

We have already mentioned the need for greater freedom in recommending use of the condom, a freedom that needs to be evidenced in practice as well as in policy.

Some consideration should be given to whether individual patients are likely to use the condom or the diaphragm more consistently.

OUT-OF-CLINIC POSSIBILITIES

If the simpler contraceptives—vaginal jellies and tablets and oral pills—prove to be medically acceptable, many possibilities for more effective family planning are opened up. Some of these possibilities may seem to bring back the traveling medicine show, but we believe that for effective work with the lower portions of the working class, out-of-clinic systems have much greater chance of success than those requiring the client to come to the clinic. One intermediate step would be a mobile unit that can move into working class neighborhoods and make the clinic more accessible. Another would be the formation of discussion groups at which a trained person explains one or another simple method to a group of women in someone's home. This technique is similar to that which some appliance and utensil manufacturers use to sell their goods. These discussion groups (or whatever else they might be called) would have the advantage of remaining close to the client's home base, of giving her an opportunity to compare her problems with those of her neighbors and thus feel more at ease, and of building grass-roots community support for family planning.

The ultimate possibility is for the clinic to move to a door-to-door basis, with an individual worker making calls much as a social case worker does (although "social worker" is an unfortunate term here because it evokes an unpopular image with many of these people). The worker would be, in essence, a door-to-door salesman of family planning. The success of various cosmetic houses among working class consumers is one indication of their responsiveness to this approach. The "in-home clinic" would have the advantages of the woman's comfort in her own milieu, of the opportunity for a more personal discussion, and of the absence of an intimidating medical atmosphere.

The worker who takes the clinic into the neighborhood probably should be either a nurse or a more vaguely defined "medical worker." For most lower working class people, the nurse probably carries sufficient medical weight, particularly when the techniques to be explained are simple. Actually, all three methods noted above are so simple that they can be explained in five minutes to a willing, unconflicted woman. The time required to assure consistent use is demanded more by the psychological issues raised for these women than by the technicalities.

On the whole, it is clear that working class people have a real interest in family planning and limitation. The professional worker who is able to approach them in terms of *their* realities, *their* understandings, *their* anxieties, and *their* values and goals, instead of simply in terms of his own technical training and middle class point of view, will stand the best chance of helping them to use effectively their own self-interest in contraception.

FAMILY PLANNING IN OTHER SOCIETIES

These findings acquire added weight when we examine family planning and limitation in societies other than our own. While much of the research on this subject in other cultures presents only a sketchy picture of the situation, the congruence of findings is noteworthy with respect to working class family planning whether in Japan, India, Jamaica or Puerto Rico.*

---

* Research studies in Puerto Rico (Stycos, 1955, and Hill, Stycos and Back, 1959) and in Jamaica (Stycos and Back, 1957) provide the fullest information on the social and psychological background of family planning. The large number of studies carried out in India are more limited

Studies show that in all these areas few couples want more than four children. Just as in the United States, the two-, three- or four-child family is regarded as ideal by most Indians, Japanese, Puerto Ricans or Jamaicans. In these areas, only a minority of the women with three or more children answer affirmatively when asked whether they want more. Similarly, the response is generally very positive when wives are asked specifically whether they would like information about how to limit their families. In Japan, Koya (1957) found that about two-thirds of a group of slum-dwellers on public relief wished to learn how to limit their families. In India, studies in six different areas yield proportions of interested women ranging from seventy to ninety-six per cent. In general, those who express no interest are women who have not yet had the number of children they wish; we note in all of these studies that while interest in limitation is high, interest in spacing children is low or perfunctory.

Yet despite their interest in family limitation, most working class couples in these societies do not manage to achieve their goals. In some areas ignorance is great and the opportunity to learn of contraception is practically non-existent. Even in Puerto Rico, where contraceptive information has been reasonably widespread, until recently few lower class couples took advantage of the available resources for family planning. In other areas, while the response to family planning programs has sometimes been encouraging, fewer couples than one might expect have responded effectively to the resources offered them. Hill, Stycos and Back (1959), in commenting on Puerto Rican family size preferences, come to a conclusion that

---

to specific attitudes and behavior and do not provide as much information on the relationship of these attitudes to general family or personal characteristics (World Health Organization, 1954; Morrison, 1956, 1957; Vasanthini, 1957; Chandrasekhar, 1959a, 1959b; Ponniah, Rao, Lazarus and Gault, 1959; Krishna Rao, 1959; and Sundar Rao, 1959). In Japan, the available studies deal primarily with practical experience in family planning programs or provide statistical information about the prevalence of contraception, sterilization or abortion (Koguchi, 1955; Ozawa, 1955; Koya and others, 1955, 1958; and Koya, 1957).

seems equally applicable to lower class couples in other cultures:

> When asked for family size preferences, responses almost invariably show a preference for the small family; but in the light of the considerable degree of inconsistency of response, it might be said that there is no . . . socially sanctioned norm for either large or small families. In the face of increasing education, urbanization, and industrialization, with attendant increases in social security benefits and higher aspirations for children, it may be that older normative and economic supports for the large family have been weakened. While it cannot be said that new norms for the small family have yet fully emerged, individuals are now freer to prefer a family size in line with other economic resources should they choose to think about the matter. This preference is not firmly anchored, however, and is easily changed by new experiences. . . . We may conclude that although nearly all Puerto Ricans recognize the desirability of the small family, they do not yet feel sufficiently strongly about it to practice birth control efficiently unless the facilitating mechanisms make it relatively easy to do so.

Two Japanese experiments, in which much was done to make it easy for couples to practice contraception regularly, suggest something of the degree of support lower class people need to become effective in family limitation. In three Japanese villages and one urban slum physicians and their assistants arranged to provide couples with contraceptive information, to discuss family planning problems sympathetically with them, to give them contraceptives, and to visit the couples regularly to encourage their continued use. Over a three-year period, the birth rate in the villages dropped from 26.7 per one thousand population to 14.6; in the slum the rate over the same period dropped from 53.9 to 16.5. These reductions were accomplished concurrently with a drop of about seventy per cent in the abortion rate in both areas.

Given the interest in family limitation expressed in all of these societies, it has been fairly easy to acquaint working class couples with the possibility of effective contraception. Moving such couples from mere interest to the active use of contraception is not easy, however. In one Indian study (Sundar Rao, 1959), it was discovered that of almost 200 couples who accepted a foam tablet contraceptive, only 69 actually used one tablet and only 25 became regular users. A large number of the non-users wanted more children and presumably accepted tablets only out of courtesy to the family planning worker. In another study involving the same contraceptive method (Chandrasekhar, 1959), its adoption was somewhat more common, but even so over one-third of the women became pregnant in less than two years. The reasons these women gave for not using contraception regularly are familiar to us: the method was too much trouble, or the woman thought she was "safe," or the husband was uncooperative, or the woman feared the contraceptive would injure her or her husband, etc.

The record of Puerto Rican couples is simliarly marked by ineffectiveness in contraception. Although over half of the working class women interviewed had used some method of limitation after several years of marriage, less than one-third had done so regularly over a long period of time; sporadic use was the general pattern. The popularity of sterilization in Puerto Rico (and Japan) is understandable in terms of the poor experience these women have with contraception; as some of our own respondents commented, sterilization comes to seem the only way out of an impossible situation. In Puerto Rico, about twenty per cent of the women interviewed had been sterilized, and of the remainder, fourteen per cent planned to be and another twenty-six per cent said they would like to be sterilized. These women frequently gave as their reasons their lack of trust in or dislike of other contraceptive methods or their husbands' objection to other methods (chiefly the condom).

Behind the dismal experience with contraception of the working class couples in all these societies probably lie many of the personality and family characteristics discussed in our study of working class Americans. It is clear that after the third or fourth child, children are not wanted, they just happen. Teaching couples that this need not occur amounts to a direct attack on some of their most deeply held beliefs about the nature of reality and about their effectiveness in dealing with it. The sense that fate governs, that one cannot successfully "go against Nature," probably lies at the base of many of the superstitious and religious concepts encountered by family planning workers in all of these societies. Such fatalistic outlooks are mentioned specifically by researchers in India (Vasanthini, 1957) and Puerto Rico (Hill, Stycos and Back, 1959). These views are often recognized to be in conflict with a more modern outlook, as the Jamaican researchers discovered (Stycos and Back, 1957), but their hold is nevertheless strong because it is built into the personality in covert and non-rational ways.

Finally, efforts to guide family development rationally are handicapped in these cultures by poor communication between husband and wife, just as they are with our midwestern lower class couples. Krishna Rao (1959) observes that patterns of "male dominance, poor communication between spouses and modesty" weaken motivation for family limitation in India, and Hill, Stycos and Back (1959) comment:

> Puerto Rican couples are poorly equipped organizationally to undertake fertility planning. They lack the skills of communication between spouses necessary to turn concordance on goals and means into consensus so they can take effective action on their family size goals.

Family planning workers throughout the world seek to disarm the "population bomb." Research on the psychosocial background of family planning attitudes and behavior suggests that the key for that disarming lies in a fuller understanding of two aspects of the problem: (1) the ego resources of the individuals involved, as these are expressed in the contending ideas of "planning" *versus* "letting Nature take its course"; and (2) the meager resources of working class husbands and wives for communication and cooperation with each other. Where family planning programs have shown some success among couples at lower social levels, it has been because they were able to supply methods that these people can manage, because the workers provided solid personal support to the couples in their desire to limit their families, and because through their repeated contacts and conversations they fostered communication between husband and wife on this subject. Where, as seems sometimes to have been the case in India, the workers have not been able to break down the barriers to communication within the family, little headway has been made in fostering contraceptive practice. While research to date has done much to indicate the dimensions of the problem, intensive work in a variety of cultures will be needed before we fully understand the psychosocial forces that contend against birth control programs.

appendix a

THE ACCEPTABILITY OF CONTRACEPTIVE METHODS TO THEIR USERS

By *Mary S. Calderone, M.D.*
MEDICAL DIRECTOR,
PLANNED PARENTHOOD FEDERATION OF AMERICA, INC.

IN DR. RAINWATER'S STUDY the term "effective user" denotes a person who uses a given contraceptive method consistently and successfully. This differs from "effectiveness" as used with regard to contraceptive methods as such, which denotes the success of that method in preventing conception. It is the acceptability of a method that plays the greatest role in determining whether or not a given user of that method is "effective" in Dr. Rainwater's sense. The following discussion of contraceptive methods therefore attempts to delineate those aspects of the various methods that may particularly affect their acceptability, rather than describe these methods from the strictly medical point of view.

METHODS FOR THE HUSBAND

Male methods of contraception are designed to stop the man's semen from entering the woman's genital tract:

a) *The condom,* or "rubber," is placed on the erect penis

ACCEPTABILITY OF CONTRACEPTIVE METHODS [*181*]

in time to collect the ejaculate. This necessitates the interruption of foreplay with some possible loss of strength of erection. If entrance has occurred before placement, the man must exercise direct will-power to withdraw and place the condom, which of course may also be put into place by the woman. The fact that either or both partners may be nervous about its possible breakage or slipping during vigorous coital play may interfere with the spontaneity of the act. Also, unless there is very adequate vaginal lubrication, the dry condom may cause some vaginal irritation and additional lubrication may be required. At the completion of intercourse the careful male must also immediately inspect the condom and inform his partner if a tear is discovered so that she can take a vaginal douche at once for additional protection.

For greatest protection the woman is also advised to use a vaginally applied contraceptive jelly or cream at the same time the husband uses the condom. This combination of methods, although supplying almost perfect protection, imposes considerable responsibility and manipulation on both partners at a time when they probably most desire to be carefree.

b) *Coitus interruptus,* or "withdrawal," allows entrance and foreplay but requires the husband to be so aware and in control of his own actions that he is able to withdraw the penis immediately prior to ejaculation so that the semen is deposited outside of the genital tract. This certainly deprives both parties of the one sensation commonly accepted to be the essential and most satisfying part of the sexual act. Tension on the part of the woman as to whether or not her husband will actually succeed in withdrawing in time must clearly operate against her own free enjoyment and participation in the act. Provided her husband can control himself for a long enough time, she is at least assured of her own orgasm prior to his withdrawal; but many women state freely that their orgasms are not as satisfactory if they do not also experience their husband's orgasm.

METHODS FOR THE WIFE

1. *Vaginal.* These are methods designed to place a chemical

or mechanical-plus-chemical barrier between the vagina and the cervix.

a) *Diaphragm or cap with jelly or cream.* Doctors recommend this method most often because it is generally regarded as the most reliable. It is not the easiest to use, however, and some women resist it for the following reasons:

Even though the diaphragm interferes little or not at all with sexual enjoyment, nevertheless it must be put into place; this involves either planning ahead when the woman is preparing for bed or interrupting sex play to insert it. Planning to insert it ahead of time may symbolize to the woman that she desires intercourse that night, just as "forgetting" to put it in ahead of time may symbolize resistance to the idea of intercourse. Thus, if she has gotten to bed and finds that her husband desires intercourse, the fact that she must get up and go to the bathroom to indulge in this procedure may cause her to move with reluctance in the hope that he will say, "Never mind, forget it."

The diaphragm requires the woman to handle her genitalia. She must prepare the diaphragm, insert it, and then reach inside with her finger to make sure that it is properly placed to cover the cervix. Also, the consistency of the cream or jelly seems "messy" to some women and over-lubricating to others.

One other disadvantage to the diaphragm is the conviction of many women that it can "get lost" inside their body. Most women are unaware of the closed structure of the vagina. The impression that the diaphragm can get lost is heightened by the fact that the woman must reach inside herself and put her finger in to pull it out. One or all of these factors may contribute to the high resistance of the poorly motivated woman to the use of this method.

b) *Creams and jellies used alone.* Many women can accept the contraceptive jelly or cream designed to be used alone because this requires no forethought, except possibly to load the applicator and place it in readiness beside the bed. If intercourse is to take place, the woman has only to reach out, even in the dark, and pick up the vaginal applicator, insert it, and press the plunger. No further manipulation is required nor is she required to touch her own genitalia except superficially. Many jellies, however, are too liquid, particularly for women who have naturally high lubrication. These women may not know that certain creams are manufactured with a more solid consistency. Thus many women complain strongly of the "messiness" of jellies, which as they melt may leak out along with the ejaculate to stain bedclothes.

c) *Foam tablets.* At the present time these are not yet widely distributed in drugstores. They are being extensively tried, however, in many areas where socio-economic levels are low. Because they are so simple to use, they are apparently quite acceptable. The only manipulation required is to moisten before insertion and most women readily accept the concept of moistening them with saliva. The tablet need only to be inserted three to five minutes before intercourse. Some women complain about the slightly warm feeling occasioned by the foaming.

d) *Vaginal suppositories.* These are in broad distribution even though their effectiveness is not at high as the foregoing methods. Many women complain of these, however, because they liquify and run off like the jellies.

With all the vaginal methods of contraception, the complaint of many women is their "messiness"; how much the semen itself contributes to this is hard to say. The fact remains that in spite of assurances that douching is not necessary and in any case should not be done until at least six hours after ejaculation, many women can hardly wait to use a cleansing douche.

2. *Oral contraceptives.* Although certain synthetic steroids have been found to be almost 100 per cent effective in controlling ovulation when taken by mouth for twenty days in the middle of the menstrual cycle, they are still in the investigational phase, available only on prescription, and should not be used except under close medical supervision.

APPENDIX A

METHODS NOT RECOMMENDED

The douche. It is interesting that a method as widely used as the douche should have so few supporters among the medical profession. Its record of effectiveness as a contraceptive is extremely low, but there are many women who will say that they have used this method and that every child was a result of their planned stoppage of its use. Inasmuch as experiments have shown that active sperms reach the cervix within three minutes of ejaculation, it can be seen why the douche is such a poor method of contraception except in emergencies, as when, for instance, a condom has broken. It is interesting that the woman who will resist self-manipulation in relation to the diaphragm method may not resist the idea of a douche.

Intrauterine devices. At this time, medical opinion in the United States is consistently against any intrauterine device such as wishbones, buttons, rings, etc. These methods, however, are extremely attractive particularly to the woman who does not want to touch herself. Because they involve only a yearly visit for insertion by a physician, in the minds of this kind of woman they are an ideal method. A few physicians, contrary to medical opinion, give in to the pleas of their patients and prescribe them.

appendix b

NOTE ON RESEARCH PROCEDURES

THIS STUDY was planned as an extension of our research on various aspects of working class life in the United States. The methodological approach was similar to that of our earlier studies and is described more extensively elsewhere (Rainwater, Coleman, and Handel, 1959). Here we will cover briefly the research questions set forth at the beginning of the study, the matters covered in the interviews, and the characteristics of the sample.

THE RESEARCH QUESTIONS

The study was to be a pilot investigation of the psychosocial factors involved in family planning and contraceptive practices by working class men and women. Because the study represented a first approach to the problem, the emphasis was on covering as broad a range of topics as possible, so that significant problems might be discovered for later and more intensive investigation.

Two broad subjects of study were covered in our plan. First, we wanted to learn about specific attitudes, motives, and habits in connection with contraceptive practices; second, we wished to learn about the psychosocial context of motives, morals, and attitudes in other aspects of family living that conditioned working class contraceptive behavior.

The research questions relevant to the first of these concerns were the following:

1. What do the working class husbands and wives know

of and think about contraception, its mechanics, physiology, and psychology?

2. What knowledge do they have of the common contraceptive techniques? What practical or psychological advantages or disadvantages do they see in each of these methods?

3. What are the important variables in the choice of a particular method of contraception? What conditions the decisions about which method or combination of methods is chosen and how systematically it is practiced?

4. What are the preconceptions and feelings about some possible new developments in contraception? What is the response to the idea of a vaginal tablet and an oral contraceptive?

Questions related to the family psychosocial contexts of contraceptive behavior were the following:

1. What family circumstances of the working class man and his wife produce attitudes, feelings, and needs affecting contraception?

2. What is the relationship between broader attitudes regarding the image of bodies and genitals, sexual relations, pregnancy, and family planning, on the one hand, and the specific activities of contraceptive practice, on the other hand?

3. What basic motives, underlying conceptions, and usable knowledge operate in the use or non-use of contraceptive methods?

4. Who are the effective and the ineffective users of contraceptives, and what makes this difference?

5. How do working class husbands and wives decide on problems of family planning, or fail to reach decisions? What is the nature of the self-definition of a user or non-user of contraceptives?

6. In all of these problems, what is the wife's image of her husband in regard to contraception both as an idea and as a practice? What is his influence, and how do her attitudes and feelings about him affect what she does? And what about the husband's image of the wife in relation to contraception?

7. What is the role of ideas about planned vs. unplanned

families, continued pregnancies, etc., within the life style of the working class family?

8. What is the attitude toward helping agencies and toward medical and non-medical personnel in connection with contraception and family planning?

SUBJECTS COVERED IN THE INTERVIEWS

The study utilized intensive conversational depth interviews. The respondents were encouraged to talk freely and to discuss whatever seemed relevant after a general topic had been raised. Several subjects were systematically covered in the interview material:

1. Detailed material on the present socio-economic status and background of the wives and their husbands. Here we concerned ourselves with occupation, education, housing, neighborhood, association membership, and religion.

2. Family relations, particularly relations with the spouse and attitudes toward children. We attempted to get at the over-all importance of children, the role of motherhood and fatherhood, and the major changes in family life since the marriage began.

3. Various notions of conception and attitudes toward pregnancy.

4. Family planning and desired family size. The extent of religious feelings and contraceptive practice were investigated.

5. Reactions to various contraceptive methods, including newer methods.

6. Information on sexual relations, before and after marriage; feelings about sexual relations as a part of marriage before and at the time of marriage; current sexual relationships, awareness of one's own and one's spouse's desires; the importance of and the satisfactions and dissatisfactions with sexual relations.

7. Material on attitudes toward helping agencies and professional people involved in telling and instructing people about contraceptive methods and their effectiveness—doctors,

nurses, druggists, social workers, and Planned Parenthood clinics.

Incorporated into each interview were several special techniques. They were used to get at attitudes and to probe subjects that involve feelings and motives not readily exposed in conversation. The main instrument used was the Thematic Apperception Test. This involves the analysis of stories that people tell about pictures they are shown. The pictures are selected to represent various life situations and problems, and the respondent tells a story about each picture and projects his point of view in the story. Analysis of each story reveals the teller's basic orientation and typical ways of feeling and of dealing with problems. It provides evidence of the way the personality is organized, probing both the conscious and the unconscious levels of personality.

We collected four stories from each respondent to TAT-type pictures. Two were from original Harvard-Murray series (4MF and 13MF) and were used to elicit responses toward heterosexual relations. Two were specially designed, one to get at feelings toward discussions with a physician about contraception and the other to stimulate ideas about husband-and-wife discussions of sexual relations.

Two interview guides were used. The first was a pre-test guide and somewhat longer than the final guide. Interviews averaged about two hours each.

TRAINING AND SELECTION OF INTERVIEWERS

The nature of the material dictated special caution in the selection and training of the interviewers. Experienced interviewers who had poise, maturity, and some sense of comfort in dealing with this subject matter were carefully selected. Instruction was intensive, and the various methods and products of contraception were explained to each interviewer. In most cases, male interviewers talked with male respondents and female interviewers with female respondents.

RESEARCH PROCEDURES [189]

ADDITIONAL DATA

In addition to a sample of working class respondents, we felt that information about Planned Parenthood clinics would be helpful. Two staff members interviewed the directors of Planned Parenthood in Chicago and Cincinnati as well as various other members of the staffs of these agencies. Observations of the clinics in session were recorded. A member of our consulting staff, a psychiatric social worker, also interviewed several obstetricians and gynecologists about their feelings and attitudes toward the contraceptive services they perform. We also thought it might be profitable and interesting to talk with psychotherapists in order to collect some anecdotal material as well as specific insights into psychopathological problems in contraception; interviews were held with six psychotherapists.

THE SAMPLE

We interviewed a total of one hundred working class respondents. Of these hundred interviews, four had to be discarded because the respondents were sterile. Approximately equal numbers of interviews were conducted in Chicago and in Cincinnati. The Chicago lower class respondents were essentially an urban working class group who were raised in the city. The Cincinnati group contains a majority of rural migrants, recently urbanized or in the process of becoming integrated in urban life. We attempted to get a representative ethnic and religious cross-section of the urban working class. The sample was a quota sample. Interviewers were assigned to particular blocks in working class areas and told to interview a certain number of respondents in particular age groups. The areas were selected so that they represented a range of ethnic composition—the sample contains respondents with Southern rural white, Mexican, Italian, Polish, and

Irish backgrounds, as well as many for whom memories of old country origins are lost.

All respondents were married, living with their spouses, and of child-bearing age. Only women under forty and men under forty-five were interviewed. Forty-six men and fifty women were interviewed. Of the men, twenty-seven classified as in the lower-lower class and nineteen in the upper-lower class. Of the women, twenty-nine were in the lower-lower and twenty-one in the upper-lower class. Twenty-five of the men were Protestant, fourteen were Catholic, two were Jewish, and five expressed no religious preference. Among the women, twenty-five were Protestant, nineteen were Catholic, two were Jewish, and four had no religious preference.

REFERENCES

ACKERMAN, NATHAN W. (1958) *The Psychodynamics of Family Life.* New York: Basic Books, Inc.
BOEK, WALTER E. et al (1957) *Social Class, Maternal Health and Child Care.* Albany, New York: New York State Department of Health.
CHANDRASEKHAR, S. (1959a) Family planning in an Indian village: motivations and methods. Paper presented at the Sixth International Conference on Planned Parenthood, New Delhi, 14-21 February, 1959. Private printing.
—— (1959b) *Report on a Survey of Attitudes of Married Couples toward Family Planning in the Pudupakkam Area of the City of Madras, 1958.* Madras: Government of Madras.
DAVIS, ALLISON (1941) American status systems and the socialization of the child. *American Sociological Review.* 6: 345-46.
—— (1946) The Motivations of the Underprivileged Worker. In *Industry and Society;* William F. Whyte, Editor. New York: McGraw-Hill.
—— (1948) *Social Class Influences on Learning.* Cambridge: Harvard University Press.
—— AND ROBERT J. HAVIGHURST (1947) *Father of the Man.* Boston: Houghton, Mifflin Co.
DE BEAUVOIR, SIMONE (1949) *The Second Sex.* New York: Alfred A. Knopf, Inc., 1953.
DEUTSCH, HELENE (1933) *The Psychology of Women—Volume II: Motherhood.* New York: Grune and Stratton, 1943.
ERIKSON, ERIK H. (1950) *Childhood and Society.* New York: W. W. Norton Company, Inc.

———(1956) The Problem of Ego Identity. In *Identity and the Life Cycle, Psychological Issues,* Volume I, Number I, 1959.

FREEDMAN, RONALD, PASCAL K. WHELPTON AND ARTHUR A. CAMPBELL (1959) *Family Planning, Sterility and Population Growth.* New York: McGraw-Hill Book Company, Inc.

FRENCH, THOMAS (1952) *The Integration of Behavior, Volume I: Basic Postulates.* Chicago: University of Chicago Press.

FREUD, SIGMUND (1898) Sexuality in the aetiology of the neuroses. In *Collected Papers, Volume I.* London: The Hogarth Press, 1949.

HESS, ROBERT D. AND GERALD HANDEL (1959) *Family Worlds.* Chicago: University of Chicago Press.

HILL, REUBEN, J. MAYONE STYCOS AND KURT W. BACK (1959) *The Family and Population Control: A Puerto Rican Experiment in Social Change.* Chapel Hill: University of North Carolina Press.

HOGGART, RICHARD (1957) *The Uses of Literacy.* London: Chatto and Windus.

HOLLINGSHEAD, AUGUST B. AND FREDRICH C. REDLICH (1958) *Social Class and Mental Illness.* New York: John Wiley & Sons, Inc.

KOGUCHI, YASUAKI, (1955) The prevalence of induced abortion in present-day Japan. In *Report of Proceedings of The Fifth International Conference on Planned Parenthood.* London: International Planned Parenthood Federation.

KOYA, YOSHIO (1957) Family planning among Japanese on public relief. *Eugenics Quarterly,* 4:17-23.

———, MINORU MURAMATSU, SAKITO AGATA AND NARUO SUZUKI (1955) A survey of health and demographic aspects of reported female sterilizations in four health centers of Shizuoka Prefecture, Japan. *Milbank Memorial Fund Quarterly,* 33:368-392.

REFERENCES

LEWINSOHN, RICHARD (1956) *A History of Sexual Customs.* New York: Longmans, Green and Co., 1958.

MEAD, MARGARET (1949) *Male and Female.* New York: William Morrow & Company.

MEIER, RICHARD L. (1959) *Modern Science and The Human Fertility Problem.* New York: John Wiley & Sons, Inc.

MORRISON, WILLIAM (1956) Attitudes of males toward family planning in a Western Indian village. *Milbank Memorial Fund Quarterly,* 34:262-286.

―――(1957) Attitudes of females toward family planning in a Maharashtrian village. *Milbank Memorial Fund Quarterly,* 35:67-81.

MYERS, JEROME K. AND BERTRAM H. ROBERTS (1959) *Family and Class Dynamics in Mental Illness.* New York: John Wiley & Sons, Inc.

OZAWA, RYU (1955) Conception control in Japan. In *Report of Proceedings of The Fifth International Conference on Planned Parenthood.* London: International Planned Parenthood Federation.

PONNIAH, S., P. S. S. SUNDER RAO, K. LAZARUS AND EDNA GAULT (1959) A report after two years' work on a rural family planning project. *Journal of Family Welfare* (Bombay), 5:No. 4, 15-21.

RAINWATER, LEE (1956) A Study of personality differences between middle- and lower-class adolescents. *Genetic Psychology Monographs,* 54:3-86.

―――, RICHARD COLEMAN AND GERALD HANDEL (1959) *Workingman's Wife.* New York: Oceana Publications, Inc.

RAO, M. KRISHNA (1959) Progress in family planning in Bangalore. *Journal of Family Welfare* (Bombay), 6:No. 2, 16-23.

RAO, P. S. S. SUNDAR (1959) Awakening Rural India. *Journal of Family Welfare* (Bombay), 6:No. 1, 24-31.

RILEY, JOHN W. AND MATILDA WHITE (1940) The use of various methods of contraception. *American Sociological Review,* 5:890-903.

REFERENCES

RUESCH, JURGEN (1946) *Chronic Disease and Psychological Invalidism.* Berkeley: University of California Press, 1951.

―――, ANNEMARIE JACOBSON AND MARTIN B. LOEB (1948) Acculturation and Illness. *Psychological Monographs: General and Applied,* Volume 62, No. 5.

SLATER, ELIOT AND MOYA WOODSIDE (1951) *Patterns of Marriage: A Study of Marriage Relationships in The Urban Working Class.* London: Cassell and Company, Ltd.

SPINLEY, B. M. (1953) *The Deprived and The Privileged.* London: Routledge and Kegan Paul, Ltd.

STYCOS, J. MAYONE (1955) *Family and Fertility in Puerto Rico.* New York: Columbia University Press.

――― AND KURT W. BACK (1957) *Prospects for Fertility Reduction in Jamaica.* Mimeographed report, Conservation Foundation, New York.

VASANTHINI, R. (1957) Acceptance of family planning in rural study. *Journal of Family Welfare* (Bombay), 3:Nos. 1-2, 14-19.

WARNER, W. LLOYD (1953) *American Life: Dream and Reality.* Chicago: University of Chicago Press.

――― AND PAUL S. LUNT (1941) *The Social Life of A Modern Community.* New Haven: Yale University Press.

―――, ROBERT J. HAVIGHURST AND MARTIN B. LOEB (1944) *Who Shall Be Educated.* New York: Harper and Brothers.

――― et al (1949) *Democracy in Jonesville.* New York: Harper and Brothers.

WHELPTON, P. K. AND CLYDE V. KISER (1946) *Social and Psychological Factors Affecting Fertility.* New York: Milbank Memorial Fund. Five volumes: 1946, 1950, 1952, 1954 and 1958.

WORLD HEALTH ORGANIZATION (1954) *Final Report on Pilot Studies in Family Planning.* New Delhi: W.H.O. Regional Office for S.E. Asia.

YOUNG, MICHAEL AND PETER WILLMOTT (1957) *Family and Kinship in East London.* Glencoe: The Free Press.

INDEX

Ackerman, Nathan, 110, 191
Artificiality of family planning and contraception, 46, 53-54
  and interruption of sexual act, 54-56

Back, Kurt W., 174, 175, 178, 194
Boek, Walter E., 7, 191
Birth control (see Contraception; Contraceptive action; Family limitation)

Calderone, Mary S., 180
Campbell, Arthur A., 23, 28, 32, 150, 154, 162, 191
Catholics (see Religion)
Chance as a determining factor in conception (see Fate)
Chandrasekhar, S., 175, 177, 191
Choosing a mate, 61-63
Coleman, Richard P., 7, 52, 82, 185, 193
Conception, ideas about, 142-149
Condom (see Contraceptive methods)
Contraception,
  "birth control" as term for, 68
  extent of, 26
  knowledge of, at time of marriage, 63-66
    by women, 64-66
  "protection" as term for, 68
  by reduced frequency of intercourse, and ideas about conception, 148
  relevance of sexual relations to, 122
  responsibility for,
    husband's, 42, 127, 139
    husband's and wife's, 124
    wife's, 20, 124, 129, 138-139
Contraceptive action,
  and attitudes toward intercourse and genitalia, 122, 139
  effective, 21, 22, 56-57
  and active rejection of sexual relations, 125-126
  and ambivalence in sexual relations, 131-134, 139
  and attitudes toward marital roles, 70-71
  and cooperation of couple, 20-21, 32, 41, 46, 123
  and father's attitude toward children, 89-91
  and ideas about conception,

INDEX

Contraceptive action *(cont'd)*
146-147
and mother's attitude toward children, 88-89
and mutuality in sexual relations, 122-124, 139
and repressive compromise in sexual relations, 128-130, 139
and self-concept of men in marriage, 81
and self-concept of women in marriage, 75-77
wife's health as an issue in, 129
ineffective, 20-21, 36, 56, 58
and active rejection of sexual relations, 126-128, 139
and ambivalence in sexual relations, 134-138, 140
and attitudes toward marital roles, 70-71
and concepts of excess fertility, 127
and father's attitude toward children, 90
and husband's attitude toward pregnancy, 85
and ideas about conception, 148
and mother's attitude toward children, 86-88
and mutuality in sexual relations, 123, 125
and self-concept of men in marriage, 80-81
and sexual relations, 37-39
sexual abandon as an interference in, 100-101
Contraceptive methods, 22
choice of, 26-28

condom, 22, 27, 37, 58, 64, 127, 135, 136, 139, 140, 150-153, 154, 156, 162, 170, 177, 180-181
and ideas about conception, 148-149
as premarital appliance, 64
diaphragm, 27-28, 124, 125, 127, 153-158, 159, 162, 163, 164, 170, 182
and education of women, 154
and ideas about conception, 146, 148
douche, 22, 27, 125, 126, 128, 162, 184
feminine appliance,
acceptance of by wives, 129, 139
and ideas about conception, 146-147
and mutuality in sexual relations, 124
rejection of by wives, 128, 139
oral, 163, 165-166, 171-172, 183
pessary, 22
rhythm system, 22, 27, 33, 55, 126, 135, 159-161, 162
use of, by Catholics, 160
and education of women, 160
and ideas about conception, 148
sterilization, 37, 135, 177
suppositories, 22, 124, 158-159, 183
and ideas about conception, 146
vaginal jelly, 124, 129, 159, 163-164, 170-171, 182-183

INDEX [199]

Contraceptive methods (cont'd)
  and ideas about conception,
    146, 148
  vaginal tablet, 124, 163, 164,
    170, 177, 183
  and ideas about conception,
    146
  withdrawal, 22, 27, 126, 161-
    162, 181
Contraceptives,
  non-users of, 28, 32-36
  and education, 28
Courtship in relation to family
  planning, 61-63

Davis, Allison, 7, 51, 191
de Beauvoir, Simone, 82, 191
Deutsch, Helene, 82, 191
Diaphragm (see Contraceptive
  methods)
Douche (see Contraceptive
  methods)
Drinking as an issue in marital
  relations, 76-77, 120

Erikson, Erik H., 51, 96, 191-192

Family limitation,
  husband's attitude toward, 32,
    37
  physician's role in encourag-
    ing, 43
  time of adoption, and educa-
    tion of wife, 26
  and the working class, 6-8
  (see also Contraceptive ac-
    tion)
Family planning,
  as an ego activity, 50-52
  motivations in, 31-32
    convenience, 31

  financial, 31, 45-47
  health, 32, 48
  family harmony, 45, 49
  patterns of
    careless group, 36-40, 58, 126
    "do-nothing" group, 32-36
    early planners, 29-32
    late, desperate group, 40-43,
      84
  and spacing, 29
  rationales for, among Cath-
    olics, 47
  relevance of sexual relations
    to, 122
  social status factors in, 24-28
  success in, 28, 30
  in urban areas, 22, 44-45, 55
  (See also Contraception;
    Contraceptive action;
    Family limitation)
Family planning programs,
  advertising as part of, 169-170
  clinic practice in, 172-173
  educational efforts in, 168-170
  methods prescribed in, 170,
    172
  out-of-clinic promotion of,
    173-174
Family size,
  desired, 24-26, 44
  and unconscious emulation of
    parents, 54-55
Fantasied birth control (see Fate)
Fate, attitude toward, as a determining factor in conception, 40, 54, 56-58
Fertility, concerns about, 19
Freedman, Ronald, 23, 26, 28,
  32, 150, 153, 160, 162, 192
French, Thomas, 51, 192
Freud, Sigmund, 1, 192

INDEX

Gault, Edna, 175, 193
"Genital" relationships, 96
God's will, attitude toward, as determining factor in conception, 40, 54

Handel, Gerald, 7, 52, 69, 82, 185, 192, 193
Hess, Robert D., 69, 192
Hill, Reuben, 174, 175, 178, 192
Hoggart, Richard, 7, 192
Hollingshead, August B., 7, 192

India, family planning in, 174-178
Indianapolis Fertility Study, 23
Interviewers, training and selection of, 188
Interviews, characteristics of the sample, 189-190
Interviews, subjects covered in, 187-188

Jamaica, family planning in, 174-178
Japan, family planning in, 174-178

Kiser, Clyde V., 23, 194
Koguchi, Yasuaki, 175, 192
Koya, Yoshio, 175, 192

Lazarus, K., 175, 193
Lewinsohn, Richard, 22, 160, 193
Lower class (see Working class)
Lower-lower class (see Working class)
Luck as a determining factor in conception (see Fate)

Malthus, 22

Marital roles,
 concepts of, 66-71
 and effective family planning, 70-71
 the good husband, 67
 the good wife, 67-68
Mead, Margaret, 6, 20, 193
Morrison, William A., 175, 193
Myers, Jerome K., 7, 193

Nature as a determining factor in conception, 54
Naturalness,
 of large families, 54-55
 of pregnancy and motherhood for working-class women, 83
Neo-Malthusianism, 22

Oral contraceptive (see Contraceptive methods)
Ozawa, Ryu, 175, 193

Parenthood,
 attitudes toward, 81-91
 and husband's feelings of masculinity, 84
 and wife's feelings of femininity, 84-85
Planned Parenthood Federation of America, Inc., 167
Planning, attitudes toward,
 middle class, 50-51
 working class, 51-53
Ponniah, S., 175, 193
Population problems, 1-3, 178-179
 in the United States, 22-23
Puerto Rico, family planning in, 174-178

INDEX

Rainwater, Lee, 7, 52, 82, 180, 185, 193
Rao, M. Krishna, 175, 178, 193
Rao, P. S. S. Sundar, 175, 177, 193
Redlich, Friedrich C., 192
Religion,
  and attitudes toward contraception,
    Catholics, 56
    Protestants, 56
  and choice of contraceptive method, 26-28
  and number of children expected,
    by Catholics, 25, 32
    and Church Doctrine, 27
    by Protestants, 25
  and use of contraception by Catholics, 35-36
Rhythm method of contraception (see Contraceptive methods)
Riley, John W., 22, 162, 194
Roberts, Bertram H., 7, 193
Ruesch, Jurgen, 7, 194

Self-concept in marriage,
  man's, in relation to wife, 77-81
  woman's, in relation to husband, 71-77
Sexual intercourse, knowledge regarding, by women prior to marriage, 66
(See also Sexual relations)
Sexual relations,
  ambivalence in, 131-138, 140
  and frequency of intercourse, 132, 135, 140
  concerns over pregnancy in, 134-138
  educational role of husband in, 110
  effect of pregnancy upon, 84
  eliminative concept of, 111-112, 118, 126, 128
    and contraceptive method, 152
  evasiveness of men about, 111
  husband's enjoyment and satisfaction in, 94-95
  as indication of marital adjustment, 92
  initiating role of man in, 93-95
  knowledge of, at time of marriage, 63-66
  mutuality in, 96-109, 121
    and contraceptive method, 154-155
    and frequency of intercourse, 97
    and ineffective contraceptive action by Catholics, 35-36
    the "loving" ones, 103-108
    the "sexy" ones, 98-103, 108
    and woman's attitudes toward husband, 107-109
  patterns of, uninterested men, 94
  prevalence of different patterns of, 121
  rejection of, 109-118, 121
    active type, 113-118
    and contraceptive method, 151-152, 161-162
    and frequency of intercourse, 109, 111, 140

INDEX

Sexual relations *(cont'd)*
  and the repressive compromisers, 118-120
  and woman's attitude toward husband, 120
Slater, Eliot, 7, 194
Spinley, B. M., 7, 194
Sterilization (see Contraceptive methods)
Stycos, J. Mayone, 84, 174, 175, 178, 192, 194
Suppositories (see Contraceptive methods)

TAT (Thematic Apperception Test), 188

Upper-lower class (see Working class)

Vasanthini, R., 175, 178

Warner, W. Lloyd, 7, 194
Whelpton, Pascal K., 23, 28, 32, 150, 153, 160, 162, 192, 194
White, Matilda, 22, 162, 194
Willmot, Peter, 7, 194
Woodside, Moya, 7, 184
Working class,
  adolescents, 52
  and public health problems, 7
  attitudes toward parenthood, 82-85
  definition of, 3-4
  wives' conceptions of husband-wife relationship, 72-73
World Health Organization, 175, 194

Young, Michael, 7, 194